ADOLESCENT WORLDS

ADOLESCENT WORLDS

Drug Use and Athletic Activity

M. F. STUCK

PRAEGER

New York
Westport, Connecticut
London

Library of Congress Cataloging-in-Publication Data

Stuck, Mary Frances.
      Adolescent worlds: drug use and athletic activity / M. F. Stuck.
          p.   cm.
      Includes bibliographical references (p.).
      ISBN 0-275-93647-3
      1. Teenagers—United States—Drug use—Case studies.
2. Teenagers—United States—Alcohol use—Case studies. 3. Sports—
United States—Case studies. 4. Drug abuse surveys—United States.
I. Title
HV5824.Y68S87   1990
362.29'08'8796—dc20   90-34288

British Library Cataloguing in Publication Data is available.

Library of Congress Catalog Card Number: 90-34288
ISBN: 0-275-93647-3

First published in 1990

Praeger Publishers, One Madison Avenue, New York, NY 10010
An imprint of Greenwood Publishing Group, Inc.

Printed in the United States of America

The paper used in this book complies with the
Permanent Paper Standard issued by the National
Information Standards Organization (Z39.48–1984).

10 9 8 7 6 5 4 3 2 1

Contents

Tables and Figure

Acknowledgments

A work of this magnitude would not be possible without the assistance of a number of different people. Thanks are extended to the adolescents who were interviewed; to the two field interviewers, Margret Ksander and Bruce Berg; and to former colleagues at Syracuse University too numerous to mention. Also to Paul Macirowski and Praeger for belief in and assistance with this work, and to Carole Berglie for her outstanding job of copyediting.

To my dog, Peanut Butter, I say "thanks" — for being there when no one else wanted to, or could be; I also apologize for benign neglect.

One person in particular is most especially deserving of recognition. My deepest gratitude and love are extended to Dr. Mary Catherine Ware, my colleague, mentor, friend, and severest and most consistent critic and supporter. Without her assistance with data entry, with library searches, with typing, with index preparation; without her continuous reading, questioning, criticizing, editing of the multitudinous versions of this work; without her patience, concern, prodding, support, love, none of this would have been possible.

This project was supported by Grant Number 84-IJ-CX-0061 from the National Institute of Justice. Points of view or opinions stated in this document are those of the author and do not necessarily represent the official position or policies of the U.S. Department of Justice.

This project was also supported by a grant from the Faculty Senate Research Committee of Syracuse University. Points of view or opinions stated in this document are those of the author and do not necessarily represent the official position of Syracuse University.

1

The Questions

Research in the area of adolescence and drug use suggests that youth who are more susceptible to boredom are more likely to engage in deviant behavior such as drug use (Adams and Resnik, 1985; Wasson, 1981), and that involvement in "alternatives which provide fulfillment, self-understanding, new experiences, or changes in emotional states" (Hobfall and Segal, 1983; Barnes and Olson, 1977:359), in structured "peer programs" (Resnik and Gibbs, 1981), in experiences that include the "development of community" (Everhart, 1982), and in activities that provide the opportunity for self-development through "individual effort and meaningful cooperation" (Sugden and Yiannakis, 1982:26) are viable methods of drug abuse prevention and/or rehabilitation.

This literature, while helpful conceptually and theoretically, both assumes that drug use equals drug abuse and imposes models, concepts, and explanations onto the experiences of adolescents. That is, much of this research addresses the issue of drug abuse either (1) without offering any definition of drug use or abuse or (2) by providing some a priori, expert, researcher-established definition of abuse, with no reference to, or input from, the individuals who are being described as using or abusing drugs, individuals whose worlds may hold meanings for the terms "use" and "abuse" quite different from those of the outside "expert," the researcher.

Equally informative would be a more interpretive, *verstehen*-oriented approach, which seeks to explore two important related areas in order to discover:

1. The ways in which drug nonuse and drug *use* (with no automatic assumption or imposition of the concept of *abuse*) fit into the lives of, and are talked about by, those youth involved in structured alternative activities,

2. How drug use/nonuse fits into the lives of, and is talked about by, those youth *not* involved in structured, alternative activities.

The current study makes no prior assumption of drug abuse nor does it explore the subjects' definitions of abuse. Rather, as an alternative, this study attempts to obtain and utilize the meanings, accounts, explanations (Scott and Lyman, 1968) of drug use offered by a sample of adolescents, in their own words. For, as Spradley (1979:13) notes: "Any explanation of behavior which excludes what the actors themselves know, how they define their actions, remains a partial explanation that distorts the human situation."

Structured, alternative activities are defined as organized nondelinquent activities, often but not necessarily school-sponsored. The activity of interest in this study is sports involvement, the essence of which lies in its formally structured, organized form (Leonard, 1984; Edwards, 1973). The justification for selecting sports as the focal activity was based upon three factors: (1) the preeminence of sports in the lives of Americans; (2) a historical belief in the efficacy of sports as a means of discouraging "delinquency" (Alvarado in Rhoden, 1984; Addams, 1974; Coleman, 1965; Educational Policies Commission, 1964; AAHPER, 1954; Strong, 1907); and (3) a preliminary analysis of the interviews that will provide the data for this book, which revealed that the single most frequently identified structured activity in which the adolescents engaged was sports.

Involvement in sports activities is seen as a type of "peer program" which affords participants the opportunity to have new experiences, to learn the meaning of "individual effort and meaningful cooperation" (Sugden and Yiannakis, 1982:26), to develop self-understanding, and at the same time to develop a sense of community via team membership (Figler, 1981:vii–viii; Berryman, 1978; Stevenson and Nixon, 1972).

Only 3.7% of the U.S. population are unaffected by sports, that is, these people do not participate in any fan or athletic activity more than once a month. . . . About seven of every ten Americans either watch sports or sports news on television; read the sports section of the newspaper; read books or magazines on sports; or talk about sports with their friends *every day.* (Research & Forecasts, 1983:7)

> Teenagers participate in sports much more frequently than any other group. Indeed, two out of every three people 14–17 years of age (66%) are avid sports participants. (Research & Forecasts, 1983:29)

Sport is an important institution that occupies a major place in the American social structure, an institution which is a major agent of socialization (Kenyon and McPherson, 1981; McPherson, 1981; Coleman, 1961a, 1961b; Gordon, 1957; Hollingshead, 1949; Lynd and Lynd, 1929). Hanks (1981) indicates that participation of adolescents in voluntary associations, first and foremost in athletics, may have very positive consequences that continue into adult life. Thus, through the process of socialization provided by sports involvement, some major societal values — self-discipline, good social behavior, emotional maturity, and stability — are thought to be realized (Segrave and Chu, 1978; Cowell and Ismail, 1962; Biddulph, 1954; Stodgill, 1948).

While it is now common knowledge that usage of various drugs is pervasive in professional sports, the popular belief still seems to hold that young athletes are, in contrast, "clean cut," "wholesome," and more likely to embody "clean living" than their nonathletic counterparts (Rooney, 1984). In fact, "another indication of the wide support for young people participating in sports is that three out of every four Americans (75%) believe that athletes are good role models for children, and 59% agree that athletes are often the best role models children can have" (Research & Forecasts, 1983:62).

The broad goal of this study is not just to explore the place of sports in adolescent society, since this can be seen in the accounts of adolescents, some of whom are athletes and some of whom are not, but also more specifically to explore the ways that drug (including alcohol) use/nonuse fits into the lives of, and is talked about by, youth who participate in sports activities and those who do not.

THE RESEARCH PROBLEM

The specific focus of this book, then, is to examine (1) the place and meaning of sport in the lives of the adolescents in this study; (2) the ways in which drug use/nonuse (alcohol, marijuana, and other drugs) fits into the lives of, and is talked about by, youth involved in the organized nondelinquent activity of sport; and (3) the ways in which drug use/nonuse fits into the lives of, and is talked about by, youth *not* involved in the organized nondelinquent activity of sport, as these are revealed in the words and accounts of the adolescents themselves.

The following, more specific questions will be examined in the chapters that follow:

1. What is the place and meaning of sports in the lives of the adolescents in this study?

2. Is the popular conception that sports and "clean living" go hand-in-hand, especially among youth, upheld or is it a myth (Rooney, 1984)?

3. What are the explanations offered by adolescents regarding their use/nonuse of drugs?

4. How do the explanations of drug use/nonuse offered by youth involved in sports compare with the explanations of drug use/nonuse by youth not involved in sports?

5. Is involvement in sports chosen by some individuals as a means by which they either seek to prevent their own drug use and/or as a means by which individuals already using drugs attempt to rehabilitate themselves? Generally, then, is sport a form of individually chosen social control (Segrave and Chu, 1978)?

6. Is such involvement in sports, rather than a mechanism for prevention or rehabilitation, a mechanism for "temperance," that is, limitation, of kind and/or amount of drug used?

7. What part does the peer group play in an adolescent's social world, specifically in relation to drug use/nonuse; and more particularly, is sports involvement merely one more type of "peer group" that facilitates and encourages or makes more difficult and discourages the use of drugs?

In sum, the major questions of the study proceed from a general theoretical concern for *verstehen* — understanding of how the actors, in this case the adolescents themselves — explain drug use/nonuse and involvement/noninvolvement in sports.

Broader Theoretical Perspectives

This study utilizes several theoretical perspectives drawn from sociology: Sutherland's theory of differential association (1939), a learning theory approach, helped to inform all of the foregoing research questions. In a related fashion, Cohen's notion of the concept of subcultures (1955) was also used. Social control theories, specifically aspects of Hirschi's (1969) control theory and Sykes and Matza's neutralization theory (1957; Matza, 1964a) were used to make sense of some of the findings.

Some observations from this study will also be related to certain theoretical issues within the sociology of sport literature. For example, the data from this study will be used to discuss the contention that sport is a major social institution (Loy et al., 1981; Lueschen and Sage, 1981; Snyder and Spreitzer, 1974) and agent of social control. These theoretical perspectives (i.e., sport as a social institution and as an agent of social control) in turn have a bearing upon more general theoretical contentions that the major institutions (family, education, sports, religion, etc.) play an important role in the maintenance of social order — that is, they are agents of social control.

IMPORTANCE OF THE STUDY

The research described herein is an important and needed addition to sociological knowledge for several reasons. First, virtually no research within the area of the sociology of sport (or within the area of substance use) has dealt with the question of drug usage among adolescents who happen to be athletes. Second, much of the research that has been done in the area of adolescent drug use has used survey instruments, which, with forced-choice answer categories, can only scratch the surface of the complexities involved in drug use. Third, little or no work has dealt with the way in which adolescents talk about (i.e., explain, justify, account for) drug usage. If social scientists and policymakers concerned with adolescents wish to produce findings that may have a positive impact upon those who are the subjects of their research, it is important to learn how adolescents talk about their activities, especially drug activities. The meaning of drug activity to youth may be quite different from how the "experts" are defining it, not only because they each belong to different speech communities (Scott and Lyman, 1968), but also because, "all scientific explanations of the social world can, and for certain purposes must, refer to the subjective meaning of the actions of human beings from which social reality originates" (Schutz, 1962:15).

In the chapters that follow, the reader will be introduced to appropriate literature in the field of sociology and the sociology of sport. The methodology for the current study will be described. Findings that address the specific questions mentioned above will be discussed, and, finally, broad policy recommendations based on the findings will be delineated.

2

Theoretical Perspectives and
Related Research

This chapter will highlight the literature in areas related to this study and will expand on the theoretical perspectives used throughout this work. The social learning theories of differential association and subcultural theory will be introduced and discussed generally; Hirschi's (1969) social control theory, and Sykes and Matza's (1957) neutralization theory will be presented in some detail. Literature in several other related areas will be reviewed: adolescent drug use/nonuse, the relationship of sports and delinquency; sport as an institution and particularly as an agent of socialization; and sports and drug use/nonuse.

OVERVIEW OF THEORIES

An overview and explanation of each of the broader sociological theories to be used will be presented here, followed by a section that presents a review of some of the research that applies these theories to the study of adolescent drug use.

The learning theories — differential association and subcultural theory — will be reviewed first. However, because of the inherently global nature of the learning theories themselves, and because of their general contribution to the more specific theories of social control and neutralization theory, there is no plan to investigate specific claims of either theory.[1] They are, nonetheless, of import because of the historical, conceptual, and theoretical contributions they make to Hirschi's control theory and to Matza's neutralization theory, both of which will be examined specifically to determine the ways in which this study informs the theories and how the theories inform the study.[2]

Learning Theories

Differential Association — Sutherland. Sutherland's theory of differential association (1939), a learning theory approach, underlies all of the research questions in this study. Learning theories "postulate the presence of both conventional and deviant socializing agents, both conventional and deviant learning environments, and bonding to both conventional and deviant groups" (Elliott et al., 1985:37). Very simply, Sutherland's theory[3] states that if an individual associates with certain types of people (e.g., athletes, delinquents), the more likely the individual is to become that type of person her/himself through the process of learning (including "techniques," values, shared meanings, often including a common special language, etc.) as a result of this association.[4] As Elliott et al. (1985:35) point out in their rather comprehensive review of the literature,

> The primary deviant learning context is the adolescent peer group; the greatest variation in normative orientations, delinquent behavior patterns, and social reinforcements for delinquent behavior are found in this social context . . . learning theory postulates that there is a direct socialization to delinquency primarily within adolescent peer groups.

This theory provides a background for all of the specific research questions of this study, since differential association as a learning theory can help to explain both routine, conventional behavior as well as routine, "delinquent" behavior, such as drug use.[5,6] Specifically, this study has utilized the broad contribution of differential association theory — namely, the notion of learning of behaviors, explanations, definitions, and so on within the context of interaction with significant others — since this is reflected specifically in Matza's neutralization theory.

The major questions of the study relate to different aspects of differential association, from the relatively straightforward issue of participation/nonparticipation in sports activities,[7] to the related notion of peer group influence regarding drug use/nonuse (e.g., what users/ nonusers learn from their respective groups), to the more complex issue of explanations and accounts offered for drug use/nonuse behaviors (e.g., the learning of rationalizations, etc., from different groups).

Subcultural Theory — Cohen. As was the case with differential association, Cohen's subcultural theory provides global, more general background to the more specific theories of concern to the study. Related to the general notion of learning theory, and specifically to Sutherland's idea of differential association, is Cohen's concept of subculture (1955). Cohen's theory (also classified as a "strain" theory), was originally developed to explain (1) the existence and content of delinquent subcultures and (2) the concentration of this delinquent subculture among the male working class of American society.

Cohen argued that delinquency[8] was characteristic of working-class boys who adopted, from their class structure, inherently negativistic, malicious, and nonutilitarian values and behaviors as a result of their being unable to achieve success as defined and measured by middle-class values (Hammersley, 1981; Siegel and Senna, 1981; Cohen, 1955). He also stated that delinquents form their own subculture based upon possession of a value system directly in opposition to the dominant culture. Cohen originally described the delinquent subculture as one that takes "its norms from the larger culture but turns them upside down. The delinquent's conduct is right, by the standards of his subculture precisely because it is wrong by the norms of the larger cultures" (1955:28). There is, however, little empirical evidence that supports this view (Elliott et al., 1985).

In this study, a more general concept of subculture, drawn out of Cohen's work, was utilized which includes the following points:

1. A subculture is a collection of individuals who possess similar or common interests, characterized by the interaction of its members.

2. Interaction with others not in possession of these shared interests is reduced.

3. Social interaction within the subcultural group(s) results in the individuals manifesting behaviors, attitudes, beliefs, and so on characteristic of the subculture (Donnelly, 1981b; Pearson, 1981; Shibutani, 1955).

It must be noted, however, that the concept of a subculture is still an ambiguous notion that includes "a wide range of relationships [and groups] and ignores important differences" (Best and Luckenbill, 1982:25; Short and Strodbeck, 1965). Also the idea of subculture within sociological literature usually and traditionally refers to "deviant" or "delinquent"[9] groups and activities, often gang behavior, and is usually used to explain the "delinquency" of the "lower class" (cf., Rubington and Weinberg, 1981; Cloward and Ohlin, 1960; Kitsuse and Dietrick, 1959; Cohen, 1955). While in this study no such traditional use of the concept of subculture is employed, the concept is still problematic in its meaning and use.

The major use of Cohen's work here is related to the concept of defining a subculture as this is reflected in social control and/or neutralization theory; this study will attempt to ascertain whether or not there were some kinds of distinctive subcultural differences between athletes (presumably "nondeviant" groups) and nonathletes,[10] whether there are subcultural differences between drug users and nonusers,[11] and so forth, as these are reflected in or can be inferred from the findings.

As this study moves to more specific theoretical perspectives, both social control theory and neutralization theory will be utilized. Control theory, in contrast with learning theories, postulates that there is a natural proclivity toward deviant behavior that occurs because of weak or absent bonds to conventional groups and norms (Hirschi, 1969).

Social Control Theories

At the outset it must be noted that the notion of control theory is problematic at best, for two major reasons. First, social control takes as givens the issues of deviance and delinquency; an assumption is made that such concepts have meaning (the same meaning?) to all who would make use of the various theories (see Meier, 1982). Second, as a result of this lack of conceptual clarity, further assumptions are made regarding which behaviors are classified as "delinquent" or "deviant," and models reflecting these unexamined assumptions are then used to explain empirical data. In sum, social control theories seem to ignore or overlook the fact that the meanings of "deviance" and "delinquency" are socially constructed, and thus there can be many meanings for each concept, not all of which are similar. It should be noted that this study attempts to avoid the problem of social construction of reality by the researcher since it does not use the concepts of "delinquent," "deviant," or "drug abuse" — all terms which can have many different meanings. Rather, this study simply examines adolescent drug use/nonuse and the adolescents' explanations for this behavior, regardless of the way this use might otherwise be labeled by agents of the various justice systems or drug educators and rehabilitators.[12]

Social control theories assume the existence of a set of commonly agreed-upon norms, violation of which is defined as deviance or delinquency. Again, the concept "norm" is not defined and explored; rather the existence and definition of norm(s) are assumed and taken for granted. Gibbs (1981) addresses at great length the problematic nature of assumptions about norms, posing questions about the issues of consensus, contingencies, and differential power in relation to norms and suggests that the "reality of norms becomes suspect" if there is not "appreciable agreement" in definitions of a norm and if independent observers cannot agree on the identification of the norms of given social units. Just as the American norm on any specific given behavior may not exist, there also exist both formal and informal versions of norms. In fact, supporting the notion of multidimensionality of norms, the data from another study using the same sample as this one revealed the existence of different norms for "right" and "wrong" behavior within different categories of youth (Berg et al., 1982).

Nonetheless, with these caveats in mind, social control theories, specifically that of Hirschi and that of Matza, will be described as useful theoretical perspectives with which to examine the data.

Hirschi's Social Control Theory. In his control theory, Hirschi (1969) maintains that "delinquent" behavior (e.g., drug use) is linked to the bond that an individual maintains with society. If the bond weakens or is broken, the individual may violate the law, since society's constraints are lifted. Without these controls which tie individuals to the society, youth reject social rules and then are free to engage in delinquent acts.

According to Hirschi there are four main elements of the social bond — attachment, commitment, involvement, and belief.

Attachment has been variously defined as: "a person's sensitivity to and interest in others" (Siegel and Senna, 1981:160); "affective ties which the youth forms to significant others" (Wiatrowski et al., 1981:525); and "the bond of affection for conventional others" (Hirschi, 1969:83), with attachment to parents, peers, and schools being most important.

Two elements of Hirshi's control theory, commitment and involvement, can be examined as a unit. Each element has been variously defined. Commitment has been defined as: "the time, energy, and effort expended in pursuit of conventional lines of action" (Siegel and Senna, 1981:161); "the aspiration of going to college and attaining a high-status job" (Wiatrowski et al., 1981:525); and "aspirations to achieve conventional goals" (Hindelang, 1973:480; Hirschi, 1969:162). Involvement is in some senses the behavioral component of commitment: "Participation in conventional activities" (Wiatrowski et al., 1981:525); and "involvement in school related activities" (Hindelang, 1973: Hirschi, 1969).

Together, these, according to Hirschi, serve as a deterrent to delinquent behavior.

Belief has been variously defined as: "the sharing of a similar set of human values and morals" (Siegel and Senna, 1981:161); "the absence of (effective) beliefs that forbid delinquency" (Hirschi, 1969:198; Hindelang, 1973); "the acceptance of the moral validity of the central social-value system" (Hirschi, 1969:26; Wiatrowski, 1981:525).[13]

In this study, these elements were utilized (with a slightly different operational definition of the concept of attachment) as part of a conceptual and theoretical framework with which to view the data.[14] For Hirschi, the *critical* form of attachment was defined as attachment to parents and family. However, this is a very limited definition of "attachment," for it fails to recognize two important facts. First, the period defined as adolescence is characterized by a number of developmental tasks that include (among others): (1) development of one's individuality, (2) formation of commitments with individuals outside the immediate family, and (3) separation from family and home and development of personal autonomy (Varenhorst, 1981; Konopka, 1973; Erikson, 1968). Each of these developmental tasks is identified as part of the process by which a youth becomes a mentally, psychologically, and socially "healthy" adolescent (and eventually adult). However, the achievement of these developmental tasks seems to run counter to Hirschi's definition of "attachment," meaning attachment to parents and family, as one of the components of the social bonding process that in turn precludes involvement in "delinquent" or "criminal" activities.[15] The adolescent developmental literature seems to indicate that "normal, healthy" adolescents are probably not attached to family in the way that Hirschi implies.[16] Thus, this measure (attachment to family) of the component of attachment in Hirschi's social control theory seems highly suspect when dealing with adolescents experiencing "normal" adolescent development.

Second, the attachment component as defined by Hirschi also fails to recognize the importance of school and peers (although Hirschi does admit that these are among the most important socializing institutions). School and peers are two facets of social life with which adolescents are most familiar and with which they spend a great deal of time, and with which and to which there is a great deal of interaction and "attachment." (Mensch and Kandel, 1988, address the relationship between attachment to school and drug involvement.) It is within the context of school and peers that many of the developmental tasks of adolescence (e.g., development of autonomy, development of individuality, formation of new commitments) are, and must be, carried out.

In this study, then, rather than parental attachment being the focal dimension, another type of attachment was focused upon — namely, involvement in sports activities that encompass attachment to peers and/or to school. By virtue of what sports participation entails, the elements of Hirschi's theory, commitment — sensitivity to and interest in others; involvement — time spent as a result of commitment; and belief — acceptance of conventional rules and values (Snyder and Spreitzer, 1980; Schafer, 1971), may be fulfilled.[17] Sports participation, especially team sports, requires sensitivity to and interest in one's teammates, belief in the rules of the game, and commitment of time and energy to practice and play, in order that the activity can be carried on. Based upon the apparent problems with Hirschi's definition of attachment when compared to the developmental tasks of adolescence, and based upon the fact that sports entails all the elements of Hirschi's theory, sports involvement was selected as the indicator of attachment in this study.

Hirschi's social control theory, in conjunction with the aforementioned more general theories, is related to the research questions mentioned in the first chapter. In addition, several of Hirschi's specific claims will be examined to determine the similarity with or differences from the findings of this study. These specific claims (Hirschi, 1969:23, 159, 190) are as follows:

1. The leisure of the adolescent produces a set of values, which, in turn, leads to delinquency.

2. There is a very strong tendency for boys to have friends whose activities are congruent with their own attitudes.[18]

3. Most "conventional" activities . . . neither inhibit nor promote [delinquency].

Matza's Neutralization Theory. Matza's (1964a; 1969; Sykes and Matza, 1957) neutralization theory posits that individuals spend their lives on a continuum somewhere between complete freedom and complete restraint in the American society, a complex pluralistic culture. Neutralization theory then, in contrast with Hirschi's control theory which sees the youthful "delinquent" as someone who has rejected social norms, holds the view that "delinquents" and "nondelinquents" share the same basic values and attitudes, since the former (i.e., delinquents) cannot be "totally immune from the demands for conformity made by the dominant social order" (Sykes and Matza, 1957:665).

Neutralization techniques are methods — specifically, justifications for behavior — by which an individual negates or neutralizes legal and/or conventional expectations for behavior. These techniques allow individuals to temporarily "drift" from commonly accepted standards and engage in "delinquent" activities. Matza and Sykes have identified five of these neutralization techniques:

1. Denial of responsibility: delinquents claim that their actions simply were not their fault.

2. Denial of injury: individuals deny the wrongfulness or harm of their actions. For example, theft of a car is described as "borrowing" or "joyriding"; vandalism is described as a prank (this is frequently reinforced by societal attitudes that "boys will be boys").

3. Denial of victim: individuals claim that the victim of the delinquent or criminal action "had it coming." For example, some youth who engage in car theft rationalize the theft by stating that any driver who leaves her/his car with the keys in it deserves to have it "borrowed."

4. Condemnation of the condemners: delinquents see what they label (correctly or otherwise) as corruption, hypocrisy, favoritism, or exceptions to the rules in the ranks of the conventional world, and claim that it is unfair for those in positions of authority to punish adolescent misconduct. For example, a youth who drinks against the wishes of her/his parents explains that the parents have "no right" to forbid drinking since they themselves do it.

5. Appeal to higher loyalties: for many youth, loyalty to their peer group (i.e., the higher loyalty) takes precedence over the rules of the larger society. For example, in response to a question about why he smokes cigarettes, one individual responds, "I smoke to be a part of the group who I associate with."

Several of Matza's "techniques of neutralization" (i.e., denial of injury, appeal to higher authority) and several of Weinstein's (1980) techniques of neutralization, based upon Matza's work (e.g., appeal to defeasibility,[19] appeal to social pressure) appear to be particularly useful concepts for this study, especially in relation to the study's questions that deal with the explanations the adolescents gave concerning their use/nonuse of drugs — explanations which may be seen as "rationalizations . . . justifications for deviant behavior . . . [which] make the deviant behavior possible" (Sykes and Matza, 1957:668). Given the major assumption of neutralization theory (i.e., that individuals spend their lives on a continuum somewhere between complete freedom and complete restraint and that in order to engage in "delinquent" acts legal and/or dominant societal expectations must be negated), and given that drug use is not an activity that falls within legal or dominant societal expectations, then by definition the reasons individuals give for drug use are "justifications" and/or "rationalizations" that negate the dominant societal and legal expectations.

Several specific claims from both Matza's neutralization theory and the works of others who have used Matza's neutralization theory will be examined for their connections to the findings of the present study. These are:

1. That much delinquency is based on what is essentially an unrecognized extension of defenses to crimes, in the form of justifications for deviance seen as valid by the delinquent but not by the legal system or society at large (Sykes and Matza, 1957:666).

2. That techniques of neutralization are critical in lessening the effectiveness of social control (Sykes and Matza, 1957:669).

3. That the most frequently used techniques are, in order, denial of victim, condemnation of the condemners, denial of responsibility, denial of injury, and appeal to higher authority (Mitchell and Dodder, 1983).

4. That delinquency and neutralization cannot be identified as general phenomena *sui generis*; rather, one must refer to the type of delinquency as well as the specific technique of neutralization employed (Mitchell and Dodder, 1983).

5. That the use of various techniques attests that the "user accepts responsibility for breaking the law but disclaims any wrongdoing" and that the users "believe indulgence is an act that is rationally chosen, pleasurable, and not harmful" (Weinstein, 1980:582).

6. That nonusers claim (among other things) that they "do not need illicit drugs, are happy with their lives, or have no desire to escape reality" (Weinstein, 1980:591).

Further, the data will be examined to determine if the accounts given for drug use fall under the classifications of explanations (specifically

Matza's techniques of denial of injury and appeal to higher authority, and the techniques of appeal to defeasibility, appeal to psychological drives, and appeal to social pressures as developed by Weinstein based upon Matza) which by definition are "justifications . . . for deviant behavior" (Sykes and Matza, 1957:668).

All of the foregoing theories are useful for the analysis of the data of this study from a conceptual and grander theoretical perspective. Hirschi's social control theory and Matza's neutralization theory will be discussed in more detail in Chapter 6 based on analysis of the findings. Given the questions of interest in this study, of equal importance is research that specifically addresses adolescent drug use/nonuse and research relating the area of sports and various delinquency theories. Literature in each of these areas is summarized in the sections to follow.

SELECTED RESEARCH RELATED TO
ADOLESCENT DRUG USE/NONUSE

As implied above, the social learning theories (differential association and subcultural theory) are the meta-theory behind the more specific theories of social control and neutralization. As general theoretical perspectives they were supported by many of the studies reported here. Mensch and Kandel (1988), Pisano and Rooney (1988), Johnson et al. (1986), Adams and Resnik (1985), American Association of School Administrators (1985), Hawkins et al. (1985), Blount and Dembo (1984), Kaplan et al. (1984), Biddle et al. (1980b), Kandel (1980), Akers et al. (1979), Levine and Kozak (1979), Ginsberg and Greenley (1978), Kandel et al. (1978), Jessor and Jessor (1977), Lucas et al. (1975), and Forslund and Gustafson (1970) indicate that involvement with peers, and the learning which occurs with and through them, have a significant effect on marijuana, alcohol, and other drug use. "Extent of perceived drug use in the peer group, self-reported drug use by peers, and perceived tolerance for use are all strong predictors of a youth's subsequent initiation into use of alcohol, marijuana, or other illicit drugs" (Kandel, 1980:269). Rugg and Jaynes (1983:17) state that chemical use of all types provides a "ready made" peer group that is a vehicle for socialization into the use of drugs. Rooney (1982), Sarvela and McClendon (1983), and Rooney (1982–83) report that there is a high correlation between peers' use of alcohol and the adolescent's personal use of alcohol, thus also supporting subcultural and learning theories.

In a related fashion, but from a slightly different perspective, the work of Biddle et al. (1980a) and Conger (1980) also supports these theories.

However, the thrust of these works is that rather than the peer group influencing the individual to use or not use drugs, specifically alcohol, the adolescent who does or does not drink will seek out and choose friends of similar habits (Biddle et al., 1980a:239–40) and "match" her/his behavior to that of the given environment (Conger, 1980:137). Related to this, Brown (1982:122) suggests that "peer pressure" comes less from the group than from the adolescent's own willingness to conform to the chosen group's norms and expectations. Chapter 4 will present data related to this issue.

Since sport is a major focal point of this study, research relating sports and delinquency using these theoretical perspectives will next be examined.

SPORTS AND DELINQUENCY[20]

It has been repeatedly stated that sport is a social fact, a major American institution that has a pronounced influence on individuals within this society, thus is an agent of socialization (McPherson, 1981; Kenyon and McPherson, 1981; Coleman, 1961a, 1961b; Gordon, 1957; Hollingshead, 1949; Lynd and Lynd, 1929) and social control (Seagrave and Chu, 1978; McIntosh, 1971). Historically, there has existed a popular belief, often with a corresponding policy implementation, that sports could act as "an effective and powerful antidote to delinquency" (Seagrave, 1983:181). Similarly, Fagerberg and Fagerberg (1976) found that sports and recreational activities were chosen as preferred alternatives to drug use. Related to this, sports have been a vital and integral part of school curricula (McIntosh, 1971; Coleman, 1965; Waller, 1965; Educational Policies Commission, 1964; Fichter, 1961; AAHPER, 1954).[21] The belief in the relationship between sports and delinquency is seen in the results of a recent study in which it has been reported that 82 percent of Americans agree that increased participation in sports would greatly reduce teenage crime (Research & Forecasts, 1983:54).

Similarly, there is the popular belief in the United States that sports build character as well as strong bodies. Involvement in sports is often felt to promote positive social behaviors and to produce "super people" who are models — in physique, in health, and in character — for the rest of the world. Novak (1976) states that sports provide for society the symbolic function of representing goodness, faith, fair play, and fun. In his seminal work, Schafer (1969a, 1969b) found that individuals who participated in sports were less likely than their nonathletic counterparts to engage in delinquency. In a later work, Schafer comments that sports involvement, particularly interscholastic sports involvement, serves "first and foremost as a social device for steering young people — participants and observers alike — into the mainstream of American life through the overt and covert teaching of attitudes, values, and behavior patterns" (1971:6). Likewise, there is often an "intuitive" sense that young athletes are more likely to embody "clean living" than their nonathletic counterparts (Rooney, 1984). In studies related to this, a number of researchers have found that athletes have a lower rate of juvenile delinquency than do nonathletes (Segrave and Hastad, 1982; Buhrman and Bratton, 1978; Segrave and Chu, 1978; Landers and Landers, 1977; Buhrman, 1977; Schafer, 1969a, 1969b). Segrave (1981b:6) states that "athletic participation has been viewed as a particularly fertile ground for promoting conformity behavior and discouraging deviant and delinquent behavior."

There are a few studies which have concluded that sports participation plays no role in deterring delinquent behavior (Yiannakis, 1981; McCann et al., 1977; Sutherland and Cressey, 1955; Tappan, 1949); that delinquent gangs often evolved from sports clubs and groups (Thompson, 1977; Thrasher, 1963); that athletic programs are characterized by self-selection of conformers (Yiannakis, 1981), hence there is less of an inverse relationship between delinquency and sports than was previously assumed (Rooney, 1984; Donnelly, 1981a; Schafer, 1969a, 1969b); that adolescents with delinquent tendencies probably would not participate in organized sports, given the structures, rules and norms of sport (Sugden and Yiannakis, 1982; Yiannakis, 1980; Glueck and Glueck, 1950); and that sports involvement may promote delinquency — for example, fighting, drinking cheating (Santomier et al., 1980; Segrave and Chu, 1978; Lueschen, 1976). Donnelly (1981a:417) concludes that "a similar type of individual may be attracted to both athletic and delinquent behavior, and that minor modifications in behavior may allow the substitution of one for the other." However, the overwhelming belief, supported by much research, is that sports participation is likely to produce appropriately socialized citizens and to deter delinquency (Segrave, 1983). Matza himself concludes "athletes are the handmaidens of convention . . . the substance of athletics contains within itself — in its rules, procedures, training, and sentiments — a paradigm of adult expectation regarding youth" (1964b:207).

Schafer (1969a:41–44) provides a theoretical grounding for the "deterrence" effect of sports which suggests that, among other things, athletes are less likely than nonathletes to become delinquent because of exposure to strong conforming influences; athletes are more likely to perceive of school as a source of success rather than of frustration; athletes' masculinity can be asserted on the playing fields and courts (authors speak only of masculinity in relation to sports, thereby reinforcing the long-standing and falsely dichotomized sexual and cultural stereotype that sports are, by definition, "manly" or "masculine"); athletes' off-the-field behavior is traditionally and typically regulated by "training rules"; athletes are less likely to be bored during their nonschool time; and athletes are less likely to be labeled as deviants and trouble makers (Segrave, 1983; Segrave and Hastad, 1982; Landers and Landers, 1977).

Research Relating Subcultural and Control Theories to Sports

In relation to social control and subcultural theories, Snyder (1972) concludes that athletes, especially those from the lower class, are greatly influenced by their coaches in terms of conforming behavior and attachment to school, and Schafer and Armer (1968:27) found that "potential dropouts who are athletes are likely to get encouragement from coaches and others, while non-athletic potential dropouts are likely to get much less encouragement, from anybody." Ferdinand (1966) concluded that athletes are subject to "many conventional influences that most adolescents never experience [and] any anti-social tendencies that exist incipiently in the athletic cliques are counterbalanced . . . with rather powerful forces of a conventional sort" (1966:125).

Similarly, some research has concluded that attachment (Hirschi's first element of the social bond) to friends among athletes serves as a deterrent to delinquent behavior (Purdy and Richard, 1983; Snyder and Spreitzer, 1979; Buhrman, 1977; Rehberg, 1969; Schafer and Armer, 1968).

Research also indicated that Hirschi's element of commitment is positively related to sports involvement, and here commitment is exemplified in several different ways (Purdy and Richard, 1983). As discussed by Snyder (1972), locker-room slogans rather vigorously promote the importance of character, hard work, and conformity. Snyder and Spreitzer (1979) found that athletes are perceived by their high school peers as behaviorally more conventional than nonathletes. Segrave and Chu (1978) indicated that the community exerts pressure on the athlete to conform to acceptable standards of behavior.

The third element of Hirschi's social bond, involvement, seemed also positively related to sports participation. Buhrman and Bratton (1978), Landers and Landers (1977), and Buhrman (1977) all found that athletes are involved in other types of extracurricular activities in addition to their sports. This lends support to the notion that an athlete has less free time and less chance to become bored, thus there may be the likelihood of less involvement with delinquent activities (Wasson, 1981; Minatoya and Sedlacek, 1979; Butler, 1976; O'Connor, 1976; Guinn, 1975; Messo-longhites, 1974; Cohen, 1973; Spady, 1971; Schafer, 1969; Clinard and Wade, 1966; Briar and Piliavin, 1965; Bordua, 1960).

In summary, Schafer's (1971) work supported the notion that organized sports, especially those that are school sponsored, promote a conservatizing influence and serve to transmit values of the status quo through emphasis on external rewards, teaching of passive acceptance of orders, and the development of "bureaucratic personalities" (Snyder and Spreitzer, 1980:135).

The findings of this study will be examined later in the book to determine whether or not individuals who participate in sports display behavior that conforms to the societal expectations of an athlete (i.e., they do not use drugs) and whether the typologies of adolescents offered by the subjects themselves reflect a distinction between those who display conventional behavior (i.e., the "jocks") and those who display, by dominant societal standards, nonconventional behavior (i.e., the "druggies"). Likewise, the data will be examined to determine whether participation in sports appeared to have tempered drug use. Through the adolescents' own accounts, the popular myth of sports as "clean living" will be explored also to see if adolescents believe in this relationship and whether or not they support it behaviorally.

Sports and Drug Use

If we turn to research dealing more specifically with drug use as the particular delinquency of concern, we find some quantitative studies have sought to explore the relationship of athletic performance to drinking and drug behavior. These studies have produced somewhat conflicting results. Hayes and Tevis (1977) found that among 10th and 12th grade students of both sexes, those who participated in athletics more often were abstainers and were less often heavy drinkers than nonathletes. Varsity male athletes were less likely to use stronger drugs. Blum et al. (1970) found that college students for whom sports were of little or no importance had more experience with all classes of drugs than those for whom athletics were important. Tec (1972) found that high school students who aspired to be the "best athlete" had low rates of marijuana use compared to those who did not aspire to excel in sports. Moos et al.

(1976), however, found that male heavy drinkers described themselves as more athletic than abstainers. Rooney (1984) found, in a study of high school seniors, no relationship between athletic participation and use of illegal drugs or alcohol. Leonard (1984), based upon work with professional male and Olympic athletes, found that drug usage within sports fell into two main areas: drugs as "restorative . . . to alleviate injury, pain, hypertension, sickness, and dissipation" and as "additive . . . to enhance performance" (Leonard, 1984:128). Where other issues of drug use have been addressed, the mode has been journalistic (e.g., *Ball Four,* Bouton, 1970) and the subjects focused upon have typically been adult male professional athletes. Little work, if any, has been done in this area using qualitative methods (e.g., ethnography, in-depth interviews, participant observation, etc.). Thus, the findings of this study promise to contribute to the body of knowledge in this area from a fresh methodological perspective, since the data are qualitative.

SUMMARY

This chapter has reviewed literature in areas of concern to this study and has discussed the social learning theories of differential association and subcultural theory; likewise, Hirschi's social control theory and Matza's neutralization theory have been presented briefly. Selected literature related to adolescent drug use/nonuse, particularly as this is related to the theories of concern in this study, to sports and delinquency theories, to sport as an institution and particularly as an agent of socialization, and to sports and drug taking, has been reviewed.

The majority of the literature seems to support the notion that sports involvement does serve as an alternative, a deterrent to involvement in delinquent activities and drug taking. Likewise, much research showing the positive relationship between sports involvement and delinquent activities has utilized the theoretical perspectives of subcultural affiliations, differential association, and control theories.

However, it must be acknowledged that many of these studies suffer from various theoretical and methodological problems, including: inadequate methodologies, reliance on official court records as the primary indicator of delinquency (which reflect only more serious offenses and/or bias against lower class and/or minority youth), differing definitions, and uses of various theoretical frameworks (Purdy and Richard, 1983; Segrave, 1983); a focus almost exclusively on males; and a lack of attention to seriousness or type of "delinquent" offense (Segrave and Hastad, 1982). Also, as stated earlier, little research has been conducted using qualitative methods (e.g., ethnography, in-depth interviews, participant observation, etc.). While this study in no way purports to correct all of these problems, it seeks to add different perspectives to the research literature by making no attempt to define behaviors as "delinquent"; addressing the lack of concern with alternative methodologies through its use of participant observation and in-depth interviews; and letting the athletes and nonathletes speak for themselves concerning their activities, in an attempt to add to the body of knowledge currently existent.

NOTES

1. Even the more specific claims (e.g., see note 3, the nine propositions of differential association) are still so vague as to be able to explain virtually anything one wished to explain. Since any theory that can explain so much may not explain anything, the fit with the data of this study (and vice versa) could be quite good, but not really informative.

2. On a grander scale, both Hirschi's control theory and Matza's neutralization theory are actually variants of learning theory, since each theory implies the learning of social/cultural values and expectations. For example, if one is "bonded" to society (Hirschi, 1969), one certainly has learned and accepted the values of society. Likewise, if one must use neutralization techniques because one cannot be "totally immune from the demands for conformity made by the dominant social order" (Sykes and Matza, 1957:665), then it follows that one has already learned what those demands/expectations are.

3. Sutherland's original statement of his theory was first published in 1939, in *Principles of Criminology,* and was refined by Sutherland and Cressey and presented in 1955, in the fifth edition of the same book. This refinement consisted of nine propositions (1955:77–80):

1. Criminal behavior is learned.
2. Criminal behavior is learned in interaction with persons in a process of communication.
3. The principal part of the learning of criminal behavior occurs within intimate personal groups.
4. When criminal behavior is learned, the learning includes (a) techniques of committing the crime, which are sometimes very complicated, sometimes very simple; (b) the specific direction of motives, drives, rationalizations, and attitudes.
5. The specific direction of motives and drives is learned from definitions of the legal codes as favorable or unfavorable.
6. A person becomes delinquent because of an excess of definitions favorable to violation of law over definitions unfavorable to violation of law.
7. Differential associations may vary in frequency, duration, priority, and intensity.
8. The process of learning criminal behavior by association with criminal and anticriminal patterns involves all the mechanisms that are involved in any other learning.
9. While criminal behavior is an expression of general needs and values, it is not explained by those general needs and values, since noncriminal behavior is an expression of the same needs and values.

4. Akers (1977) refined Sutherland's basic theory by adding the notion of differential social reinforcement of behaviors. Thus the decision to engage in certain behaviors ("conforming" or "deviant") is a result of the perception of the rewards or costs, the social reinforcements for given behaviors. Even with the addition of this notion of calculation and resultant behavior, Akers' refinement of Sutherland's differential association theory is still a social *learning* theory (see the title of his 1977 book).

5. "Delinquent" is put in quotes to emphasize the fact that application of the label of "delinquent" is dependent, not upon the fact or act of drug use, but upon who it is that is doing the labeling. The adolescents who use drugs in this study do not define their drug use as "delinquent," although traditional theoretical statements do.

6. See note 1.

7. The works of Buhrman and Bratton (1978); Segrave and Chu (1978); Segrave (1981a); and Schafer (1969a, 1969b) all attest to the differential association of athletes, but tie this association to class issues, as is the case with traditional differential association theory.

8. The use of terms such as "deviant," "deviance," "juvenile delinquency," and "delinquent" behavior is beset with problems, given the various definitions and measures that have been used to indicate these. Segrave (1983) emphasizes the fact that "juvenile delinquency" is an official term used by agents of the criminal and juvenile justice systems, while "delinquent" behavior may be "deviant" behavior and may or may not come to the attention of the agents of the various justice systems.

Gold (1970:4), in fact, has suggested that the notion of the "delinquent" ought to disappear since it has been shown empirically that nearly everyone from time to time breaks laws, thus making everyone "delinquent" or "deviant." The importance, he suggests, is that there are differences in the frequency and seriousness of the "deviation," thus "delinquency" should be seen as a matter of degree. He also makes the point that, in fact, "delinquent behavior" is a traditional part of adolescence.

9. See note 7.

10. There are a number of works that have identified an "athletic subculture" (e.g., Donnelly, 1981b; Snyder, 1972; Rehberg, 1971, 1969; Coleman, 1961a, 1961b).

11. Huba et al. (1979:265) found that "adolescent drug users do *not* appear to form subcultures delineated from non-user subcultures along interaction dimensions other than that of drug use" (emphasis added).

12. Of course, it can be said that the adolescents' own descriptions or explanations of drug use are definitions that constitute a social construction or reality, but this is the adolescents' *own* reality, as described by them.

13. Much of the available research indicates that the belief component is the weakest of the four in terms of predicting behavior (Johnstone, 1981; Meade and Marsden, 1981; Krohn and Massey, 1980; Johnson, 1979; Empey, 1978; Thomas and Hyman, 1978; Hirschi, 1969).

14. Hirschi's study methodologically used measurement and correlation, and thus his findings are not directly useful for comparison with the findings of this study, since the findings of his study are presented statistically and quantitatively, and the findings of this study are presented qualitatively. However, the development of the components of commitment, involvement, attachment, and belief are conceptually and theoretically useful.

15. If attachment to parents is assumed to preclude involvement in "delinquent" activities, and if adolescent drinking is classified as a "delinquent" behavior, it is interesting to note that one study (Kwakman et al., 1988:252) finds that "one of the drinking attitudes is significantly related to the quality of the attachment relationship with the parents, i.e., drinking alcohol to facilitate social contact. Adolescents . . . particularly mentioned drinking for this purpose most frequently."

16. Hirschi's notion of "attachment" to parents also fails to account for involvement in "delinquency" by adolescents who are attached to their parents.

17. Acceptance of conventional rules and values is fulfilled directly through the essence of sport and indirectly through the acceptance of school, where the sport is school-related or school-sponsored. Waller (1965) and Nolan (1955) found that participation in athletics produced school attachment. Related to this, Schafer and Armer (1968) found that athletes are more likely to see school as a positive rather than as a negative experience. However, Segrave (1981a, 1981b) found that athletic participation did not produce school attachment, and concluded that athletics in and of itself is not a deterrent to delinquency, but rather that commitment to "conventional" society rather than simply to athletics must be fostered.

18. At the same time that Hirschi makes this statement he also says that "no good evidence has been produced to show that attachment to peers is actually conducive to delinquency" (1969:84). If the "leisure of the adolescents produces a set of values, which, in turn leads to delinquency" (1969:23), one assumes that these adolescents are attached to one another; otherwise, how do they share the values? If this is so, then what is the meaning and logic of Hirschi's statement that there is no evidence that peer attachment facilitates delinquency?

19. "Defeasibility" is a term used by Weinstein (1980:580) to refer to excuses which assert, either directly or indirectly, that the users [of drugs] "have 'knowledge' about the possible harmfulness of illicit drugs and the 'will' not to use them, but that societal circumstances or one's social situation [e.g., peer groups] make usage probable."

20. The term "delinquency" is used for this section heading because it reflects the foci (and usually the titles) of the studies reported here. Drug use (usually only marijuana and/or alcohol) is nearly always one of the types of delinquency included, but is seldom the only "delinquency" investigated.

21. Sports programs were also integral components of the nineteenth-century British juvenile correctional systems (Tappan, 1949; Healy and Alper, 1941; Segrave, 1983). In the current American prison system, some facilities support and develop teams, particularly in basketball and baseball. Both prison and juvenile detention facilities encourage and provide time for "exercise" even if team sports are not allowed.

3

Methodology

The preceding chapters have presented the research questions for the study and have reviewed relevant literature related to these questions. This chapter will briefly describe the overall research design: the data collection, coding, and retrieval procedures and the data analysis procedures. This chapter will also present a summary of descriptions of all subjects based upon the conceptual schema developed for this study.

There are two different research designs, one a subset of the other, used within this project. The Yule City Study is the "parent study," from which the data used in this particular research come. A description of the Yule City Study will be presented, followed by the more specific design and techniques used for this research dealing with adolescents, drugs and sports involvement.

BACKGROUND: YULE CITY STUDY

The Yule City Study is one of a set of interconnected research projects on drug use and criminal activity funded by the National Institute of Justice and conducted by the Interdisciplinary Research Center for the Study of the Relation of Drugs and Alcohol to Crime.

The Yule City Study employed principally a qualitative, ethnographic design with emphasis upon participant observation and in-depth interviewing, which resulted in the collection of vast amounts of rich qualitative data related to a variety of issues. At the same time, the design also incorporated positivistic traditions in the form of a scheduled interview format and in a specially designed mainframe computer program for assistance with data analysis and retrieval. More detail on the Yule City Study may be found in Appendix A.

DESIGN FOR STUDY: ADOLESCENTS, DRUGS, AND SPORTS

The areas of interest for this study were focused differently and were more specific than those of the "parent" Yule City Study. The conventions developed for the Yule City Study were not adequate to the task of this study, thus a new system was developed to facilitate the retrieval and analysis of data pertaining specifically to the areas of concern for this study of adolescents, sports, and drugs. Before that system is described, the process by which this particular study was conceived and developed will be presented.

Sample for this Study

A pilot study was completed using a random sample of 20 of the total 100 transcripts, allowing findings, including the categorization scheme of athlete/nonathlete to emerge in true qualitative fashion. These categories were based upon the discussions of the adolescents themselves — those who were active in sports were categorized as athletes.[1] Those who were not involved with any sports activities at the time were categorized as nonathletes. (The classification schema for the complete study are discussed in the last section of this chapter.) Of these twenty, half of those interviewed had been or were involved with sports and half indicated no participation in sports. Given the theoretical assumptions concerning the relationship between sports participation and development of "good character" and "clean living," as suggested in the literature (Chapter 2) and popular knowledge, the concept of theoretical sampling (Everhart, 1982; Hammersley, 1981; Ostrander, 1970; McCall and Simmons, 1969) was utilized, and further analysis was undertaken to ascertain what factors were indicative of conformity with, or divergence from, these relationships and assumptions. Specifically, the twenty interviews were further analyzed to reveal the level of involvement or noninvolvement with various drugs and alcohol, as indicators of these theoretical assumptions. Again, the accounts of the adolescents themselves were used, and the categories for level of involvement were derived from these discussions.[2] These preliminary findings, then, based upon classification of the subjects by participation or nonparticipation in sports and the subjects' accounts of involvement/noninvolvement with and explanations of drug use (rather than by level of involvement in drugs and/or crime, as in the larger Yule City Study),[3] served to confirm the feasibility of exploring the complete data set (i.e., all 100 transcripts) using this conceptual schema.

Coding and Microcomputer Retrieval of Data

Although Yule City's mainframe computer program (see Appendix A) was used to ascertain target pages for data for this study, it was necessary to read all of the pages of all of the transcripts in order to note all relevant data, given the more specific focus of this study as compared to the foci of the Yule City Study itself. Similarly, a more detailed coding schema related to the specific focus of this study was developed, based upon the themes that emerged from the data of the pilot study, and was refined upon further reading of the transcripts.

After reading and coding each transcript, the codes from each transcript were entered into a microcomputer-based data management system. The design of the system allowed for the inclusion of codes for several types of information, with parallel fields for each substantive area (sports involvement, marijuana, beer, liquor, hard drug usage). Information included: (1) basic demographic data — transcript number, sex, race, age, grade in school (if it could be determined), and religion; (2) classification as to participation in sports, reasons for participation, which sports participated in, where or from whom the subject got her/his ideas about the issue; (3) categories of marijuana, beer, liquor (other than beer), and hard drugs, so that subjects could be classified by type of use of each of these substances; (4) a field for codes for reasons for use of each of these substances; and (5) another field for where or from whom the subject got her/his ideas about the substance. The capabilities of the data management program and the design of the form also allowed for the inclusion of any and all relevant quotations for each of the substantive areas (sports, marijuana, beer, liquor, hard drugs) and codes related to the content of the quotes (i.e., what type of themes were exemplified by the quotation).[4] For example, for the following excerpt pertaining to drinking:

Q: Do you have reasons for not drinking?

A: It just hasn't come up yet. My friends don't drink that I know of.

Q: Do you think that it's [drinking] wrong?

A: Um, too much drinking is. But I don't think it's good for kids to drink in seventh or eighth grade and ninth. First of all, you're not supposed to drink when you're that age, so.

The thematic areas include: reasons (for use/nonuse); peer groups (in reference to "My friends don't drink that I know of"); no opportunity, no desire respectively (in reference to "It just hasn't come up yet"); general fear (in reference to "I don't think it's good . . ."); illegal (in reference to "you're not supposed to drink when you're that age").

It was then possible to retrieve from the data management system whatever combination of themes the researcher wanted, including relevant quotations from all transcripts entered (e.g., printouts of all quotations from white female athletes in junior high school who never drank liquor and whose reasons included fear of losing control of themselves). The advantages of utilizing such a system include:

1. A constant comparative method. One must initially read entire transcript pages in order to select the quotes (in context) and do initial coding, then one reads the pages again while entering the selected data (i.e., the specific quotes), then upon retrieval one reads again, not simply single pages from a transcript(s), each with one or possibly two quotes of concern amid other data, but rather a whole printout of all the quotes related to a given theme (e.g., use of speed[5] for purposes of enhancement of physical performance).

2. The capacity to give a count of the number of forms in which a particular theme occurs.

3. The ability to refine and further specify codes and forms to meet one's particular research agenda.

4. Independence from the mainframe computer (e.g., down time, priority queues, etc.).

Grander, more methodological and theoretical benefits of the microcomputer retrieval process include the fact that it maintains the integrity of the qualitative method and qualitative data by allowing the analyst to focus upon the concern for discovery and the generation and development of theory particular to the foci of this study, to learn about the culture of those being studied, and to attend to the context of the adolescents' accounts by being able to read discussions in context (Hammersley, 1981; Ostrander, 1970; Glaser and Strauss, 1967).

DATA ANALYSIS

As parts of lengthy discussions about their lives and their activities, respondents spoke about their own and their peers' participation/nonparticipation in sports and their own and their peers' use/nonuse of drugs. Passages pertaining to drug use/nonuse and to participation/nonparticipation in sports were identified and analyzed using standard inductive content analysis procedures (Krippendorff, 1980; Spradley, 1979; Holsti, 1969; Glaser and Strauss, 1967), coded, and entered into the data management system. While the questions cited at the beginning of this work helped to guide the data analysis, standard qualitative analysis procedures (Glaser and Strauss, 1967) also allowed for the possible emergence of other related themes of import. As mentioned above, the data management system allowed for retrieval of the various themes that will be presented and discussed in the following chapters.

Since the findings are qualitative, the data are presented, as far as possible, in the words of the adolescents themselves. The use of the adolescents' own words is important and beneficial because their own words and language better convey *their* sense of their worlds, their behavior, and their meanings (not the researcher's). The use of the youths' own words also reveals the complexity involved in their explanations, activities, and social worlds in ways that simple quantitative tallies from surveys or simplistic percentage statements cannot. Selections included are those that are representative and typical; that is, the selections exemplify the point being made, but they are from neither the most nor the least articulate individuals. Similarly, excerpts are used only if there were no conflicting statements on the same topic elsewhere in the transcript (unless this very contradiction was the point being made, and that would be noted). Where and if warranted and justified, comparisons by gender, sports participation/nonparticipation, level of schooling (e.g., junior or senior high school), and/or drug use type and level are also presented.

In order to determine which data will be included for presentation, the questions Wiseman (1974) uses as a consideration of the significance of a finding in qualitative research will be employed, namely:

1. Is it significant because it affects a great many people?
2. Is it significant because it illustrates or reveals something of a more general (and significant) nature about human behavior? (Wiseman, 1974:326)

In conjunction with these questions, the use of Becker's (1958) and Becker and Geer's (1960) and Lazarsfeld and Barton's (1955) notion of "quasi-statistics" allows the collection and presentation of data that are implicitly numerical, but which neither require nor allow precise quantification. Thus, for purposes of this study the "criterion of adequacy" will consist of the answers to Wiseman's two basic questions, which will be taken as evidence of how typical and widespread given responses are within and among categories of youth in this study. By using the notions of Wiseman, Becker, and Lazarsfeld and Barton, it is possible basically to avoid the imposition and use of quantitative measures on qualitative data. However, for those more quantitatively oriented, if a type of response (i.e., theme) was found in the accounts of 20 percent of the subjects within a given category, then that thematic response type was considered adequate for inclusion as an account or explanation; likewise, if a given thematic response occurred in at least 20 percent of any category of the sample or within the sample as a whole, it was considered to have met the criterion of adequacy.

In terms of Wiseman's second question, it is difficult to truly and definitively know about human nature. For example, while an excerpt from an individual who states that he changed his peer group to one that used drugs in order to "show my parents that they can't be the ones to tell me what to do with my life" [#136][6] may be the only one like it numerically, it may be significant because it "illustrates or reveals something of a more general (and significant) nature about human behavior" (Wiseman, 1974:326). While any such findings are not numerically great enough to constitute a reported theme, such excerpts that seem to reflect theoretical issues, findings, or suggestions concerning human nature and/or behaviors may be included for presentation, especially where they appear to have potential bearing on further theory development (a goal of qualitative research) and/or policy recommendations. For example, related to the above excerpt, Jessor (1982) and Rugg and Jaynes (1983) indicate that drug use often plays a key role in the developmental transition of adolescence and may be an adolescent's statement of independence from her/his parents, thus the above-mentioned excerpt would be judged as worthy of inclusion because of its contribution to existent theory.

However, before the findings can be presented and discussed, it is necessary to present a description of the adolescents whose accounts are the data from which emerge the themes related to athletic participation and to the use/nonuse of drugs (including alcohol).

SUBJECT DESCRIPTIONS

As was mentioned earlier, information was compiled from ethnographic observations of approximately 700 youths in the community;

subsequently, a sample of 100 youths, ages 12–20, many of whom were involved in drugs and crime, was selected for purposes of in-depth interviewing. (See Table 3.1 for a summary of their demographics.) Of these, 36 were female; 64 were male.

Analysis of the data from these subjects indicates that levels of drug use and of crime in this sample are similar to rates that would be predicted by findings in larger national surveys of drug use by the adolescent population (Johnston et al., 1982). Similarly, despite a smaller sample size, the levels of drug use among the 40 randomly selected youth (from the total sample of 100) are virtually identical to levels in a 1978 survey conducted in Yule City (ODAS 1978). In short, the subjects in the sample appear very similar in their behaviors to other youths sampled in larger surveys.

Table 3.1
The Sample (N = 100)

Characteristics	N
Sex	
Male	64
Female	36
Ethnicity	
White	73
Minority	27
Ages	
12-13	13
14-15	39
16-17	31
18-20	17

Through the process of reading their accounts, the researcher categorized the adolescents on a number of different continua pertaining to the following characteristics: participation/nonparticipation in athletics; substance use/nonuse including, consumption/nonconsumption of beer, consumption/nonconsumption of liquor (including wine)[7]; use/nonuse of marijuana and hashish; and use/nonuse of hard drugs. The continua utilized are derived from the youths' discussions and are used as a convention for classifying these adolescents. Thus, this section will describe the various continua associated with each of the aforementioned characteristics, and will present descriptive data regarding the adolescents in terms of these characteristics.

Participation in Athletics

The accounts of the youth provided much information pertaining to sports involvement, and it was from these accounts that the continuum of activity related to this characteristic was drawn. A number of specific questions within the interview schedule elicited responses that include accounts of athletic involvement. These questions had to do with how a subject spent her/his spare time; what she/he liked to do in general; in what, if any after-school activities, the subject engaged. Accounts of athletic participation were also found in various other discussions, in response to a variety of different questions (e.g., questions about early memories, things done with the family).

From these accounts, for the purpose of this study, three clusters on a continuum of athletic participation were identified and utilized: nonathlete, recreational athlete, and organized athlete.[8] For purposes of determining assignment of a given subject on this continuum, the type of involvement coded referred to the subject's athletic participation[9,10] at the time of the interview and/or during the preceding year. Definitions of these categories and a report of the numbers of youth who fall into them follow.

Nonparticipation in Athletics: The Nonathlete. Operationally, a subject was classified as a nonathlete if she/he made no mention of sports or athletics as something in which she/he engaged, or specifically denied sports as an activity in which she/he engaged. Based upon this definition, out of 100 subjects, 40 individuals (40%) were found to be nonathletes; of these, 21 were female, 19 were male.

Participation in Recreational Athletics. A subject was classified as participating in recreational athletics if she/he indicated sports or athletics as something in which she/he engaged, but not as a part of any type of organized team, at the time of the interview or during the preceding year. Utilizing this definition, which emerged from the accounts of the youth themselves, 24 of 100 subjects could be classified as participating in recreational athletics (e.g., roller skating, swimming — mostly female; primarily basketball for males). Of those 24 recreational athletes, 18 (75%) were male and only 6 (25%) were female.

Participation in Organized Athletics. Finally, a subject was classified as participating in organized athletics if she/he indicated sports or athletics as something in which she/he engaged, on some type of organized team, at the time of the interview or during the preceding year. Utilizing this definition, 36 of the 100 subjects could be classified as participating in organized athletics, and here a noticeable gender difference appears. Of the 36 individuals engaged in organized sports, only 9 (25%) are female compared to 27 (75%) males. Table 3.2 presents a summary of athletic involvement utilizing all categories; Table 3.3 presents a summary of athletic involvement using only the dichotomy of athlete/nonathlete.

Given the themes as they emerged from the accounts of all the youth, and based upon the other characteristics of concern (e.g., drug/alcohol use/nonuse, reasons given for use/nonuse), the recreational athletes were more like the athletes than nonathletes and thus, for purposes of this study, these 60 individuals (recreational and organized athletes) have been classified as athletes. For purposes of presentation of the themes in the following chapters, only two categories on the continuum of sports

Table 3.2
Subjects by Sex and Level of Sports Involvement

Sex	Organized	Recreational	Nonathlete
Female (N= 36)	9	6	21
Male (N= 64)	27	18	19
Total (N= 100)	36	24	40

Table 3.3
Subjects by Sex and Sports Involvement/Noninvolvement

Sex	Athlete	Nonathlete
Female (N= 36)	15	21
Male (N= 64)	45	19
Total (N=100)	60	40

involvement will be utilized: nonparticipation in athletics (N = 40) and participation in athletics (youth involved in either recreational or organized athletics, N = 60).[11]

Substance Use/Nonuse

A continuum pertaining to substance use was also derived from the adolescents' discussions and is used as a convention for classifying these adolescents in terms of beer and liquor use; marijuana and/or hashish use; and hard drug use. The derivation of this continuum was a bit trouble-some owing to the very content of the adolescents' discussions.[12] None-theless, based upon those discussions, the following continuum was derived and was used for each of the categories of substance in question: nonuse, experimentation, occasional use, regular use. These will be defined below.[13] For purposes of determining assignment of a given subject to this continuum, the type of involvement coded refers to the subject's substance use at the time of the interview and/or during the preceding year.

Nonuser. Operationally, an individual was classified as a nonuser of a given substance if she/he indicated that she/he had never used or tried any drug or if she/he had never tried or drunk any form of alcohol. Subjects who had used substances but quit usage earlier than the time of the interview or the year preceding and currently defined themselves as nonusers were also classified as nonusers.[14]

In terms of beer, out of 100 subjects, only 20 individuals (9 females, 11 males) indicated that they had never drunk beer. There were no adolescents who were former drinkers of beer. Nonusers of wine numbered 19 (7 females, 12 males); nonusers of liquor numbered 31 (9 females, 22 males). This included 3 former drinkers (all male).

There were 28 nonusers of marijuana (12 females, 16 males). There were 45 nonusers of hashish (17 females, 28 males); this included 3 individuals who said they had quit using the substances (2 marijuana, 1 hashish; 2 females, 1 male). As far as other drugs[15] were concerned, there were 43 individuals who indicated that they had never tried or used any type of other drug (18 females, 25 males).[16]

Experimental User. Operationally, an individual was classified as having tried a given substance if she/he indicated that she/he had used a substance only four or five times ever. This limit was derived from the essence of the adolescents' own discussions as a kind of natural cutoff point, for it appeared that youths who used a given substance more than this in fact used it "occasionally" (see description below). There were 13 individuals who indicated that they had tried beer (6 females, 7 males); 16 who had tried liquor (5 females, 11 males); 49 who had tried wine (20 females, 29 males).[17]

In terms of marijuana and hashish, 16 individuals indicated trying marijuana (8 females, 8 males); 25 individuals indicated trying hashish (10 females, 15 males). As far as the harder drugs were concerned, 28 (11 females, 17 males) indicated trying speed; 24 said they tried acid (6 females, 18 males); 31 indicated trying cocaine (7 females, 24 males).[18]

Occasional User. An occasional user was operationally defined as an individual who reported having used a given substance less than three times per month at the time of the interview and/or during the preceding year, but more than the four to five times total for experimentation. Again, this convention was derived from the essence of the adolescents' own discussions, since this limit of less than three times per month emerged as a natural cutoff between "occasional" use and "regular" use (to be defined in the next section). Twenty-six individuals indicated occasional use of beer (10 females, 16 males); 16 indicated occasional use of wine (5 females, 11 males). There were 38 occasional users of liquor (16 females; 22 males).

As far as marijuana and hashish were concerned, there were 10 individuals who reported occasional use of marijuana (4 females, 6 males). Sixteen individuals (6 females, 10 males) reported occasional use of hashish. Across all hard drug categories, there were a total of 17 occasional users: 10 individuals indicated occasional use of speed (3 females, 7 males); 5 (1 female, 4 males) occasional users of acid; 2 (male), of cocaine; 1 (male), Quaalude; 2 (1 girl, 1 boy), Valium.

Regular User. Operationally, an individual was classified as a user of a given substance if she/he indicated that she/he used a particular substance more than once a week or four or more times a month at the time of the interview and/or during the preceding year (again, these cutoff points are derived from the essence of the adolescents' own discussions). Out of the 100 subjects, 40 (10 females, 30 males) reported regular beer consumption; 14 (5 females, 9 males) reported regular liquor consumption; only 5 individuals reported regular wine use (2 females, 3 males).

Regular marijuana users numbered 45 (11 females, 34 males); regular hashish use, in addition to regular marijuana use, was reported by 4 males. The number of regular users of hard drugs is minimal. In total, 10 youth claim to regularly use one or more hard drugs. The breakdown of regular use by substance is: speed, 8 (1 female, 7 males); acid, 4 (all males); cocaine, 2 (both male); Quaalude, 2 (both male). There was one subject (male) who also reported regularly using various other drugs (e.g., codeine, inhalants, barbiturates). Tables 3.4 and 3.5 summarize the types of use of the various substances.

Given the themes as they emerged from the accounts of all the youth, and based upon the other characteristics of concern (e.g., drug or alcohol use/nonuse, reasons given for use/nonuse), the occasional substance users were more like regular users than either trial or nonusers and thus, for purposes of this study, these individuals (occasional and regular users) have been classified as users of substances (i.e., of beer, liquor, marijuana and/or hashish, or hard drugs). Thus, for purposes of presentation of the themes in the following chapters, only two categories on the continuum of substance use will be utilized: nonuse of a given substance (the nonuser and the experimenter) and use of a given substance (which includes occasional and regular use).

SUMMARY

This chapter has presented a description of the overall research design, including data collection, coding, and retrieval procedures; data analysis techniques; and subject descriptions based upon the conceptual schema that guided this study.

The substance used most frequently by these adolescents was alcohol, either beer or liquor. Sixty-six percent were users of beer, 52 percent

Table 3.4
Degree of Substance Use

Substance	Regular	Occasional	Tried	Nonuse	Total
Beer	40	26	13	20	99*
Liquor	14	38	16	31	99*
Marijuana	45	10	16	28	99*
Hashish	4	16	25	45	90**
Wine	5	16	49	19	89**
Hard Drugs[1]	10	17	29	43	99

*Total equals 99 because data are missing from one transcript (female).
**Totals are less that 99 because data on this category are missing from several transcripts.
[1]Includes: Speed, Acid, Cocaine, Valium, Quaaludes, PCP, Inhalants, Mescaline, Opium, Codeine, Heroin, Darvon, Peyote.

were users of liquor, 21 percent were users of wine, 55 percent were users of marijuana, and 20 percent were users of hashish. The overwhelming majority (72%) of the adolescents were nonusers of hard drugs. These numeric descriptions are provided simply to give a background description of the frequency of reported involvement or noninvolvement.

The following chapters will present substantive accounts and reasons for involvement/noninvolvement in the various activities that have emerged from the discussions of these adolescents. As far as possible, these will be presented in the words of the youth themselves.

Table 3.5
Type of Substance by Use/Nonuse

Substance	Use	Nonuse	Totals
Beer	66	33	99*
Liquor	52	47	99*
Marijuana	55	44	99*
Hashish	20	70	90**
Wine	21	68	89**
Hard Drugs	27***	72	99

*Total equals 99 because data are missing from one transcript (female).

**Totals are less that 99 because data on this category are missing from several transcripts.

***This is the total of individuals who used any hard drug.

NOTES

1. During the course of various discussions, many of the youth who were involved with sports called themselves and/or their sports-involved friends "athletes." For example:

Q: Do your friends smoke or drink?
A: No. They athletes too. [#138].

2. This procedure, indeed the design of this entire study, is a significant contribution methodologically and substantively, for no studies dealing with drug use and sports participation could be found in which the primary data source was ethnographic accounts. As mentioned in Chapter 2, nearly all of the previous studies in this area have been quantitative. However, two studies dealing with delinquency generally (Biddle et al., 1980b; Gold, 1970) did use in-depth interviews, but in both the data were converted to quantitative format for manipulation and statistical presentation. (Gold occasionally also did present some excerpts from the interviews.) A study by Everhart (1982) dealing with "goofing off" in school did use in-depth interviews and did use these data for presentation purposes.

3. For purposes of this study, information specifically related to crime and criminal activities (e.g., burglary, assault, shoplifting) will not be included in the data to be analyzed.

4. The design of the form provided for some redundancy in coding (e.g., codes for "reasons for use" and codes for the "themes within the body of the quotes"), giving the ability to check and verify the themes and codes.

5. Speed is an amphetamine, an "upper" used by the youth. The term is used by youth to refer both to "real" speed and to substances such as caffeine pills.

6. Numbers in brackets — for example, [#136] — refer to transcript numbers.

7. "Liquor" refers to all types of hard liquor (e.g., whisky, gin, vodka, etc.).

8. The decision to use these categories allowed the inclusion of *any* mention of various athletic and physical activities (using conventional, commonsense notions of what were athletic activities, which allowed the inclusion of such things as bike riding) without having to employ a researcher-imposed definition of what precisely was "sport" and "athletics" and what was not.

9. If an individual had quit an organized sport, for example, but indicated involvement on a recreational basis, that individual was classified as a recreational athlete rather than as a nonathlete. If no indication of current involvement was given, then the individual was categorized as a nonathlete.

10. If an individual's accounts revealed participation in both recreational and organized athletics, the convention adopted was to categorize the individual as one who participated in organized athletics.

11. Likewise, the attempt to divide the sample further (e.g., organized, recreational, former, nonathlete) would result in numbers too small to be of much meaning.

12. Where discrepancies and inconsistencies existed among various accounts of substance consumption, a decision as to the classification of a subject was based upon assessing all of the relevant discussions and utilizing the categorization that predominated in terms of number of times similar accounts for the behavior in question were given. (For example, if in some part of her/his discussion, an individual said she/he had only tried a given substance, but in subsequent discussions and in responses to direct questions the individual revealed that she/he in fact engaged in other than trial of a substance, the subject was categorized, not as an experimenter, but as whatever type of user these other discussions revealed.)

13. For purposes of this study, the concern is not with the quantity of a substance used, but rather with the fact of using or having used it.

14. Individuals who had quit using the various substances prior to the time of the interview or the year preceding it were classified as nonusers because, in reading the discussions, these individuals were more like the nonusers than the users of the various substances in the reasons they gave for current nonuse. Some may argue that those youth who had quit using substances are not like nonusers in that the former have had actual personal experience from which they draw their reasons, while nonusers have not had that experience. However, the concern here is with similarity in what was said, since categorization was based on the substance of the adolescents' accounts.

15. The category of hard drugs (other drugs) includes 11 types of controlled substances that are not marijuana and hashish; that is, PCP, LSD-halucinogens, tranquilizers (Valium), amphetamines (speed), barbiturates, codeine, inhalants, cocaine, heroin.

16. As can be the case with any statistics, these numbers can be slightly misleading, since for purposes of these categories only a subject who had never tried *any* hard drug is counted as a nonuser.

17. Nearly all of the trying of wine was done in the context of family ritual (e.g., holidays, with meals) or special occasions (e.g., birthdays).

18. Other than adolescents who were able to be identified as never having used hard drugs (N = 43) and the few (N = 8) who indicated regular use of a number of hard drugs, any attempt to count the number of individuals who experimented with or occasionally used hard drugs is at best misleading, for in some cases, a few individuals may have tried numbers of different drugs; in other cases, larger numbers of individuals reported having tried only one hard drug each. If numbers must be employed at all, it is better to speak of the number of instances of experimentation with hard drugs, in which case there are approximately 100 codings for trials of various drugs. Since by definition the experimental category of substance use means no more than four or five times ever per subject, the actual number of trials could range from 100 to 500, while the actual number of individuals trying any hard drugs would be no more than thirty at most.

4

Adolescents' Social Worlds

The preceding chapter included descriptions of the subjects in this study plus the criteria and schema for classifying drug use and nonuse and sports involvement and noninvolvement. This chapter will briefly discuss the larger social worlds of the adolescents in this study and will elaborate on two of the focal characteristics of concern: sports involvement/noninvolvement and peer groups.

SOCIAL WORLDS OF THE ADOLESCENTS

Obviously, given the ages of the youth in this study and given that most of them are still students, school is a large part of their social world. Both the athletes and nonathletes in this study found school to be basically "OK" (i.e., neither particularly outstanding nor particularly bothersome) and only a few indicated that they really liked school. However, nonathletes more than athletes seemed to characterize school as boring.

Since school does not occupy all of an individual's time, various questions were asked that dealt with the use of free time generally, use of time with friends, and use of time after school, all of which were designed to elicit information about the social worlds of these youths. Responses to these specific questions and other types of discussions revealed a variety of different activities that occupied the free time of these youth. A total of forty different types of activities were recorded from these discussions. For example, such things as listening to music, talking with and being with friends, going to parks, watching TV, smoking ("getting high") or drinking, and "hanging out" were frequently mentioned activities in the social worlds of the adolescents, by both athletes and nonathletes, females and males. Since there were some marked gender differences, Tables 4.1 and 4.2 display activities by gender.

Table 4.1 presents the top-ranking activities mentioned specifically by females in response to questions about how the individual spent her free time or how time was spent with friends. Those listed were mentioned by at least 20 percent of the females in each of the categories of sports participant/nonparticipant. Table 4.2 lists the top-ranking activities mentioned specifically by males in response to the open-ended questions about how the individual spent his free time or how time was spent with friends. Those listed were mentioned by at least 20 percent of the males in each of the categories of sports participant/nonparticipant.[1]

While several of the top-ranked activities mentioned by both females and males are the same (i.e., talking and being with friends, hanging out, and listening to music), these tables also reveal that, in terms of top-ranked activities mentioned by the youth in this study, there appear to be some noteworthy gender differences. For example, the females appear to be more sedentary than the males; listening to music, watching TV or movies, reading or writing, singing or playing musical instruments, and shopping were among their most frequently mentioned activities. On the other hand, males mentioned drinking, smoking marijuana, getting rowdy, and playing sports among their top-ranked activities. Thus, in some respects the social worlds of the youth in this study are very much alike; in other respects, there appear to be some differences in the activities that occupy their social worlds.

However, the one prominent difference in the social worlds of the males was between athletes and nonathletes. This difference was involvement in sports: Almost exclusively, those youth who were classified as athletes mentioned participation in sports as an activity in which they spent time generally or spent time with friends. Of male sports participants, 71 percent mentioned playing sports in response to questions about the use of one's time (the largest percentage reported for any use of time). Other noticeable differences in the activities between male participants and nonparticipants were that a higher percentage of sports nonparticipants than participants (50% vs. 24%) mentioned "hanging out" and mentioned "drinking" (45% vs. 27%) as activities in which they spent their free time. As far as female participants and nonparticipants were concerned, the most noticeable difference was that female nonparticipants mentioned watching TV or movies more frequently than did female sports participants (47% vs. 20%).

Table 4.1
Top-Ranking Activities — Female
(mentioned by at least 20% of participant category)

	Friends: Talk, Be With	Hang out	Dance, Sing, Play Instrument	Listen to Music	Watch TV, Movies	Shop	Go to Park	Read/Write
Female Participants (N=15)	50%	**	27%	27%	20%	**	**	20%
Female Nonparticipants (N=20)*	69%	26%	**	26%	47%	26%	26%	37%

*Nonparticipants equal 20 because data are missing from one transcript.
**Not mentioned by at least 20% of participant category.

Table 4.2
Top-Ranking Activities — Male
(mentioned by at least 20% of participant category)

	Friends: Talk, Be With	Hang out	Play Sports	Drink	Smoke Pot	Listen to Music	Get Rowdy
Male Participants (N=45)	39%	24%	71%		37%	22%	*
Male Nonparticipants (N=19)	55%	50%	20%	45%	35%	35%	25%

*Not mentioned by at least 20% of participant category.

These findings reveal, on the one hand, that athletes appear to be quite similar to their nonathletic counterparts. Yet, on the other hand, the findings reveal that those classified as athletes are different from those classified as nonathletes by virtue of (and perhaps only by virtue of) participation in sports. In addition the observation that involvement in sports seems to be a major part of the lives of athletically involved youth is supported by two additional findings: Over 25 percent of the athletes (mostly those involved in organized sports) indicated sport as a kind of life goal (to be fully explained below), and over 35 percent of the athletes (again, mostly those involved in organized sports) indicated that sport occupied much of their free time.[2]

Sports Involvement: Place and Meaning of Sports

Some level of sports involvement appears to be a significant fact in the lives of many of the adolescents in this study, since 60 percent of them[3] were classified as being involved in either recreational or organized sports. The remaining 40 percent of the youth in this study were classified as nonparticipants in sports; however sixteen (40%) of these were individuals who had been involved in sports prior to the time of this study. This compares with findings from a recent nationwide study in which 62 percent of all those between ages 14 and 17 indicated a high interest in sports participation; in fact, 66 percent of all those ages 14 to 17 years were reported to be avid sports participants, with an additional 29 percent as moderate sports participants (Research & Forecasts, 1983:29).[4]

This section will discuss the place and meaning of sport in the lives of the adolescent sport participants and nonparticipants. It will address specific themes related to sports involvement: as life goal, as a means of occupying time, and as a vehicle for interacting with and making new friends.

Place and Meaning of Sports: Life Goal. If sports were an activity in which the adolescent reported she/he planned or hoped to be engaged as an adult, usually as a professional career, that athlete was classified as having sport as a "life goal." Twenty-three percent of all the athletes mentioned sport as a life goal, and only *one* was a female.[5,6,7] Occasionally the life goal was limited specifically to acquisition of a college scholarship; and for one individual, it was even more general — she simply looked to "future involvement with softball." It is also interesting to note that, of the individuals who indicated some form of sports involvement as a life goal, half were black,[8] evidence perhaps of acceptance of the cultural myth that sports will offer a means of upward mobility to blacks (Coakley, 1978; Edwards, 1973; Figler, 1981; Scott, 1971; Loy, 1968; Orr, 1969; Thompson, 1964).

Some of the individuals who spoke of sports involvement as a kind of life goal did so quite simply, especially in response to a direct and specific question about life ten years from the time of the interview or about the individual's goal in life. For example:

I want to be a soccer player (professional). [#015]

I always, I always dreamed of playing professional — oh, not football, just a professional sport. [#019]

Other individuals elaborated a bit more on their ideas of sport as a life goal, both articulating the career path and realizing that the goal might not be achieved, as evidenced by the following excerpts:

I'll be playing pro football. Go all the way — start from amateur and all the way to college, to the pros. [#023]

I was interested [in a sport career], but right now let's [?]. I don't really know. Um, well, when I was younger, I guess, it's, I don't know. It's just like a typical boy. All you dream is just to play sports — pro sports. Well, when, you know, now that I got older and stuff, I just realized, you know, well, if you don't get, if you don't get pro, in a sports career, it ain't that bad, you can always go to college and do something else, you know. [But] I would like it still, yeah. [#147]

Even an individual who was a recreational athlete expressed longing for a sports career at the same time as he acknowledged some of the problems of attaining it:

Well, the future I had planned as, I wanted to be a professional football player, wanna have a big house, you know, a lot of money, enjoy life, go places I never went before.... Goal in life would be like a dream, like, football, that's what I always, that's what I wanna be, bein' a football player, good athlete, ya know, football is my trainin' and I suppose one of these days I get there, it's gonna be like two or three hundred people in the line try out, gonna be hell of a lot more, and ya gotta be real good go get there so. [#130]

These discussions of sport as a life goal attest to the fact that sports do have a special place and meaning in the lives of the youth so involved, both in the present and for the future.

Place and Meaning of Sports: Use of Free Time. Evidence of the fact that sports do have a special place and meaning in the lives of the youth so involved, more specifically limited to the present temporal dimension is the mention of sports involvement as a way in which one spends one's time, and as an activity that leaves one time for little else. When asked various questions in the interview about how one spent her/his time, 35 percent of the athletes (almost exclusively the organized athletes) indicated sports involvement as a way time was spent; 81 percent of these were male.[9] The following are typical excerpts indicating that sport occupied much time in the lives of such individuals:

I usually play sports a lot. I, I play almost all the time, soccer, or something else . . . sports, yeah. That's what takes up most of my time, sports. [#015]

Sports, most of my time is in sports . . . I plan as a big part, to get part of a scholarship, in football. [#029]

And, it's hard, 'cause there's so many things I wanna do, I'm takin' like performing arts, ya know, I like acting a little, and I like all kinds of sports, and it's hard, 'cause ya can't do everything ya wanna do. You jes have to, you know, find time. [#150]

Although no longer a participant in organized athletics, the following comment by a former gymnast is also illustrative of how much time the sport had occupied in this individual's life:

Q: Do you think your childhood was average?

A: No, not really . . . there aren't very many [kids] who, um, can do, handle going to gymnastics every day after school for five hours and then coming home and doing homework. And, um, at that time a lot of kids were saying, how can you do that? You don't have time to even watch cartoons on Saturday? You don't have time to even be with friends. And, um, it doesn't really bother me because, um, not always are my friends busy. They are usually with me, and, um, actually I didn't care for the cartoons on Saturday. [#129]

Sports were a major activity in the lives of many adolescents who were identified as athletic participants, and the immediately foregoing excerpts attest to the pervasiveness, for them, of the time spent in sports.[10]

Place and Meaning of Sports: Friends. While spending time and being with friends was one of the important aspects of the social world shared by sports participants and nonparticipants, having friends who participated in sports was of importance only to the athletes in this study.[11] In contrast with sport as a life goal, a factor with a future time component, the importance of friends involved in sports is very much a "here and now" theme. This is, then, another factor attesting to the place and meaning of sports in the lives of the adolescents. The following excerpts are typical of comments about friends and sports:

> [I'm involved] in sports, football team, and the track and the basketball . . . all I usually do is sports. I say I play a good deal of, we're [friends] doing all the time is spend on sports. I like sports a lot . . . I meet them [special friends] from sports activities. [#021]

> Well, I like to play soccer, and in school I'm on the track team, and we did really good, we were unbeaten, so I thought that was pretty fun . . . track in the spring . . . I see friends cause we're in sports. [#014]

Friends are an important dimension of any adolescent's life, and sports provide a structure in which friends can be made, and within which friends can and do interact. As the above examples attest, some of the youth were aware of and able to elaborate about sports as a vehicle for meeting and being with friends.

Place and Meaning of Sports: School. For some of the youth in this study, sports (either in the form of organized team sports or as school activities in physical education) were a most meaningful factor as far as school was concerned. For some, in response to questions about school, gym was the main thing the individual liked about school and was often ranked as one of the individual's favorite subjects. While not mentioned by as many of the athletes (11% of all athletes; N = 7) as other factors related to sports, the school-sport connection is reported here for it appears to be an important one for the youth who mentioned it. The following excerpts are typical:

Q: What do you like about it [school]?

A: The students and, ah, the activities, and all the sports there. Yah, we have a basketball team, we play like fifteen teams; that's a lot

of teams for a year, ya know. And it jes be fun, travellin',
Andersonville, places like that, ya know. [#042]

Sports. . . . Gym was my favorite subject. [#036]

For one interviewee, sports occupied a special place and meaning
within the context of school: It was sports, specifically the fact that the
football coach was his math teacher, that motivated the individual not to
miss school:

A: I was involved with, um, well from the beginning of the year I
was involved in football, after school, then after that, I would
use the computers for my own recreation.

Q: Um hum. Didn't you have any trouble when you'd be out of
school all day and then you'd show up for football practice?

A: Well no, because, um, my math teacher is my football coach. So
if I wasn't at math I wouldn't go to football. But, during football
season I usually didn't miss school.

Q: Um hum. How come?

A: Well, I felt like, um, I'm a good football player, I don't think I
should lose football. So I felt, I should go to school, and then be
able to play football. So I'd do that. I basically just stayed until
after math class, and then leave school. And then come back for
football.

Q: What would you have done if the math class was later in the
day?

A: Maybe I wouldn't have left school then, and then come back to
school.

Q: Do you think that if you had been interested in other sports that
were in other seasons, like lacrosse or something like that, you
would have done the same thing if, um, you were taking a
course with one of the coaches?

A: Um hum. [#136]

This individual's comments are important for they reveal the fact that
sport was something quite important in his life.[12]

The preceding sections offer explanations and evidence supporting the
notion that sport has a definite and important place and meaning in the
lives of those adolescents who are involved in sports, especially
organized sports (since nearly all of the youth who talked about the

themes mentioned above were participants in organized sports). However, at the same time, it should be kept in mind that although sports involvement was the most emphatic aspect of the social world of the adolescents in this study which distinguishes the sports participant from the nonparticipant, the other major activities that occupied their worlds were mentioned by both participants and nonparticipants in sports (e.g., listening to music, talking and being with friends, going to parks, watching TV, etc. See also Tables 4.1 and 4.2). Thus at this point from the findings of this study, it appears that in terms of the activities of their social worlds, youth who are involved in sports and those who are not involved in sports differ mainly on that one dimension — sports involvement.

Noninvolvement in Sports

Reasons for noninvolvement in sports were somewhat varied and, if articulated at all, were articulated principally by two types of youth: youth who were nonathletes with no prior sports involvement, and adolescents classified as nonathletes at the time of the study who had been participants prior to the time of concern in this study.

Among the youth who were nonathletes, the only recurring reasons given for noninvolvement in sports were that the individual simply "did not like" sports, or that the person found them "tiring and boring."[13] These reasons were stated by one male and seven females.[14] Other than these reasons, youth who were not involved in sports basically did not elaborate upon their lack of involvement.

Nonathletes who had previously been active in sports often explained that a school change (sometimes accompanied by other reasons) was the reason they no longer participated:

Not any more . . . I was a real jock. I was in, at Elmwood I was at, at soccer two years and volleyball one year, and track one year . . . it's harder to get accepted into a new place; it has its stamp, people who've been there always who are known — I didn't feel like fighting. [#114]

This was the reason most frequently given by nonathletes who had previously been active for not currently being involved in sports.

Other than the statements about not liking physical activity generally and/or sports activity specifically, it is difficult to determine much about the place and meaning of sports to youth who are nonathletes, since those youth (at least in this study) did not talk much at all about their noninvolvement.[15,16]

With the foregoing analysis of the social worlds of the adolescents, and in particular, the fact of sports participation or nonparticipation having been presented, there is yet another aspect of the social worlds of the adolescents that is of import. This remaining dimension is that of the peer group. The following section will briefly discuss the peer group generally, but the thrust of it will focus upon the peer group as it relates to substance use/nonuse. The section presents excerpts from the adolescents' own discussions, since these reveal accounts and explanations of substance use and descriptions of their peers and friends within the context of substance use and nonuse.

The Peer Group: General Findings

The pervasiveness and importance of the peer group is germaine to the other major questions of the study. Although the literature often refers to the peer group as an influence upon an adolescent's activities (Rugg and Jaynes, 1983; Rooney, 1984; Sarvela and McClendon, 1983; Rooney, 1982–83; Resnik and Gibbs, 1981; Norem-Hebeisen and Hedin, 1981; Varenhorst, 1981), there exists in this literature a major difficulty, usually not carefully examined, concerning the concept of peer group. It is extremely difficult to determine separate cause and effect (Rutter and Giller, 1983); that is, do youth engage in a certain activity (or activities) and then choose a particular group of friends because the group members also engage in that activity? Or does an individual belong to a group whose members subsequently have somehow influenced the individual to engage in a given activity because the other members of the group do? Likewise, whether the peer group explanations and references offered by adolescents came before the act or as a justification after it is unknown, and perhaps unknowable. It is because of this problem that, in this chapter, the notion of the peer group is deliberately discussed in terms of its association with or relationship to various activities, especially substance use/nonuse, rather than as an influence upon those activities, unless influence is clearly detectable within the adolescents' own discussions (Brown, 1982; Biddle et al., 1980a; Conger, 1980).[17]

As might be expected from commonsense knowledge of the everyday life of adolescents, and from the psychological and sociological literature, peers and friends are a most important factor in the worlds of adolescents, and were mentioned by all of the respondents in this study in a variety of contexts. As was shown earlier in this chapter, when asked about what they "like to do in general," an overwhelming majority of the youth, both female and male, responded with some variation of being with peers ("hang out at my friend's house"), spending time with peers ("go to the beach with my friends"; "have a good time"), talking with friends ("talk with my friend on the phone"; "shoot the shit"), or hanging out (with friends). Playing sports with friends was the top ranked of all the activities, with 71 percent of the male sports participants indicating that they used free time for this purpose. Only four individuals were noticeable for their lack of emphasis upon peers and their mention of liking "to be alone" and "to think." As was shown earlier in this chapter (Tables 4.1 and 4.2), there do not appear to be major differences in the social worlds of the adolescents except by sex. Next to playing sports, involvement with friends was the most frequently mentioned way adolescents of all categories spent their free time.

In statements about use of free time and substance use/nonuse, in almost all cases there was a similarity between the adolescent's peer group members' use/nonuse and the adolescent's own use/nonuse of a given substance. In nearly all cases, according to the respondents' accounts, if a youth was a regular user — for example, of marijuana — most members of her/his peer group were also reported to regularly use marijuana. This same association held for all user types (e.g., regular user and nonusers) across all substances (e.g., marijuana, alcohol, hard drugs). For example, from a nonuser, "None of my friends drink or smoke or are on drugs or anything like that" [#019].

The data from the adolescents' discussions indicate that the vast majority of their substance use, trial and nonuse occurs within the context of a group of friends and/or acquaintances (Mensch and Kandel, 1988; Pisano and Rooney, 1988; Silverman, 1987; Hawkins et al., 1985; Blount and Dembo, 1984; Jackson and Jackson, 1983).[18]

Users: Respondent and Her/His Peers. Users of the various substances reported that their friends and peers also used the substance under discussion. Quite frequently, they also indicated that not only did their peer group members use the drug, but that the peer group served as the impetus for the individual's starting to use the substance. This information was offered both in response to specific questions ("do your friends use . . . ?") and in the context of the individual's explanations of her/his own use. For example, in terms of alcohol, the following is a representative comment:

Q: So, drinking is really something you like to do with your friends; why?

A: Jes, better with your friends. . . . Then you can get rowdy, and start, we can go out and do somethin' or somethin' . . . I started drinking with my friends. [#049]

Alcohol users also indicated that much of their drinking was done at parties where peers were present; users also indicated the reason for drinking (often, but not always, at parties or in small groups) was simply to get drunk with friends (to be mentioned further in Chapter 5). For example, "Um, just, like on Friday nights, we'd just get — if we were, we'd like, get a six-pack, and get — you know, split it between two people. On the weekends, you know. Just get ripped, everyone gets ripped on the weekends" [#037].

As far as marijuana use is concerned, nearly everyone smoked in or with a group (even those who indicated that they sometimes smoked alone also smoked with peers). As was the case with alcohol, friends were mentioned as using the substance and as the reason the individual started smoking. The following are typical of comments about friends and marijuana smoking:

Q: Well, tell me about it [first smoking pot]; how'd it happen?

A: I dunno, jes seen everybody else smokin'; my friends asked me if I wanted to get high.

Q: It was at a party, right?

A: Ya, so I said, why not, ha — [#035]

My friend always had pot and she got me high. . . . Everybody keeps just keeps me high — when it's around you smoke it. [#018]

Most of the respondents offered very little specific detail about their peer group and its relation to their substance use, other than to indicate that they used the substance under discussion with friends, often, but not always, at a party; used it because friends had it; and/or increased use because it was available from friends. This last point was a very important factor for many of the youth who indicated that they themselves did not keep marijuana, but rather smoked it in the company of, and because, their friends had it.[19] Very few individuals made use of the specific term "peer," although several did, in a manner similar to the following, "I just smoke it [pot] with — maybe because of peer pressure and maybe because I en — enjoy it myself" [#136].

In summary, for the users of alcohol and marijuana, the peer group was an important factor in their use, from initiation to continued use. Friends and peers were almost always mentioned in the context of the individual's own alcohol and/or marijuana use.[20]

Experimenters and Occasional Users: Respondent and Peers. As far as experimentation and/or occasional use of the various substances were concerned, peers were a major factor; sometimes a party was the specific setting mentioned. For others, no particular setting was mentioned, other than that the individual was with her/his peers. The following are representative comments about peers in the context of having tried or occasionally having used alcohol, marijuana and hard drugs.

Well, I drink it whenever, whenever my friends are having a party I'll drink; but it's not something I go out and do all the time. [#148]

Um, if somebody's — if I feel like getting high and someone's got pot, then I'll smoke it with them. I don't really get high that much now. [#143]

I used speed because I wanted to stay up because of something. I was really beat, everybody says speed keeps you awake, so I did a couple; and oh, I was wide awake . . . got them from a friend and my sister. [#020]

Again, as with all other categories and substances, elaboration was basically absent; most references to peers were simple factual statements concerning the providing of the substance and/or circumstances and/or information related to the situation in which the trial or use occurred.

Nonusers: Respondent and Peers. As was the case with those adolescents who did use various substances, or who had tried the substances, the peer group was also a factor for those youth who did *not* use any of the substances in question. Nearly all of the youth who did not use substances had friends who did not use the substances.

When asked about not drinking, the following are typical responses of those individuals who did elaborate upon the factor of peers and alcohol nonuse:

I've tried beer and some vodka . . . it felt alright, but. I just never did it again. And I just, you know, know to myself that, you know, you don't, you know, need to have that, so you know. I just, didn't do it . . . being with friends that don't do it, you know help you. [#021]

It just hasn't come up yet. [My] friends don't drink that I know of. [#024]

As far as marijuana nonuse was concerned, individuals who elaborated upon their peers' nonuse gave a specific kind of reason for that nonuse:

No, I don't think so [that friends use marijuana]. I think some of them are bright enough not to use it. [#129]

They athletes too. Most everybody on street's athlete. They run track, cross-country, somethin' like that. [#138]

Adolescents who did not use hard drugs were emphatic in their statements about their own unwillingness to "hang around" with people who did use drugs and about their friends' nonuse.

None of that garbage at all . . . we don't. I told all my friends, I said if you're going to do that, then you're not going to be my friend. They said, "no, I'm not going to do that at all." And they didn't. I Wouldn't touch that stuff. [#019]

A: I just don't like people — I don't hang around with people that use that stuff.

Q: What kinds of people do you think use drugs?

A: Kids that are bad in school. Um, don't play no sports, uh. That's it. [#109]

Again, as was the case with alcohol and marijuana, when asked about their own and their peers' use/nonuse of other drugs, the number of individuals who elaborated upon this theme of the peer group was few, but their responses are noteworthy for the strong convictions contained therein, and also for the references to sports and athletes as being connected with nonuse of drugs (reflecting the opinion that sports and "clean living" go together).

An Exception: Nonuser Respondent/User Peers. Nearly all of the nonusers indicated that their peers were also nonusers of the substance in question; however, a few of the nonusers did have peers who used the substance (usually marijuana or hard drugs) under discussion. The following is a typical comment, reflective of the theme of the "Just Say No" campaign (LeMonn, 1987), concerning marijuana use/nonuse:

Like me and my friends will be around and after school, right, and then they will take it out, right, and they'll start smoking some and I'll just leave . . . cause I don't want to get involved with it. I just don't want to get involved with this, something like that. [#025]

The following are representative of comments about an individual's nonuse of hard drugs, even though her/his peers do use these:

Q: Do you have any particular reason for not using these drugs?

A: Stuff like that [hard drugs], I don't think so [don't think I'd use them], cause I'm happy as I am — I don't need drugs to make me any different. [#127]

Q: Do you have any particular reason for not taking drugs?

A: Well, I kind of like myself, I'd like to keep it just that way. [#132]

The explanations of the adolescents (although only a few in number) who fall into this category are enlightening, for most seem to reveal choice and a strong sense of self on the part of the adolescent, especially given the importance and strength of the peer group as it is reported to influence the individual's substance use (Pisano and Rooney, 1988; Silverman, 1987; Johnson et al., 1986; Adams and Resnik, 1985; American Association of School Administrators, 1985; Hawkins et al., 1985; Elliott et al., 1985; Blount and Dembo, 1984; Biddle et al., 1980a; Conger, 1980; Jessor and Jessor, 1977; Kandel, 1974a, 1974b).

Changes in Peer Groups

The foregoing sections have dealt with several dimensions of the relation between the usage patterns of peers and the adolescents in this study. This section will address a slightly different perspective in that it will present the explanations of individuals who had made a conscious choice to change peer groups for drug-related reasons and who articulated this during their discussions. While the number of adolescents who articulated an awareness of peer group differences and their own decisions in regard to peer group choice was limited, the accounts these individuals give is of import for the content contained therein, namely an indication of rational, calculated decision making on the part of the adolescent in her/his pursuit of a particular goal — whether that goal was substance use or nonuse.

Several youth indicated a change to a peer group that was related to the individual's increased usage of marijuana and/or alcohol:

> I used marijuana so much that it's pitiful ... you can mark marijuana down [on interviewer's chart] at least three times a week since I've moved here ... I just started hanging around with them ["druggy" crowd], you know, little by little, cause once you start smoking pot and somebody asks you, you know, or something. Pot people can pick out pot people, do you know what I mean? [#012]

> *Q:* In what ways have you changed [since elementary school-aged]?

> *A:* Well, um, finding different friends, the ones who do get high, a lot, and drink a lot. And don't get along, and don't listen to their parents. And, um, losing the kids who, who are the ones who do listen to their parents and if they do drink, they know exactly how much, and everything. That's the ways I think I've changed.

> *Q:* How come? Why do you think you've changed in that direction?

> *A:* Just, um, to show my parents that they can't be the ones to tell me what to do with my life. [#136]

This latter quote clearly shows a choice on the part of the adolescent to change his peer group. However, based upon the discussions of his drug and alcohol use, it is apparent that this individual's choice of peer group was not necessarily to facilitate his own increased usage (for he had only tried marijuana and a few of the harder drugs, and only occasionally drank beer or alcohol). Rather, the deliberate choice of new peers appears to be, in a sense, an attempt to send a message to his parents, a message related to his need to be independent of their directives (cf. Varenhorst, 1981).

While the excerpts from these two adolescents exemplify change to a peer group more actively involved in the use of marijuana in particular, individuals remarked about changing peer groups in order to attempt to curtail their own substance usage, or indicate a curtailment of use because of the group with which they newly associated:

> Now, I try to only smoke on the weekends, but it's kind of difficult. And I'm changing the people I'm hanging around with now. I'm trying to hang out with kids who don't party. Cause I don't want to do it no more ... I just don't want to party no more. I'm not that

kind of person. I've had my fun with it. Shit, I don't need it no more. No, I just don't want to do it no more. [#115]

I drink less now cause I don't hang around the same people I used to. [#018]

Although the foregoing excerpts are general statements concerning peer group change, the type of peer group specifically and most frequently mentioned in relation to a decision to curb or cease substance use is one whose members are involved in sports activities.

Sports Peers and Sports as Influence Against Substance Use

The belief that having peers involved in sports and/or sports involvement itself as an influence against substance use is supported, in several different ways, by evidence from the discussions of some of the youth in this study. These findings parallel similar beliefs held by professional and collegiate athletes, (Wasson, 1981; Minatoya and Sedlack, 1979; Butler, 1976; O'Connor, 1976; Guinn, 1975; Messolonghites, 1974; Connie Hawkins in Wolf, 1972).

Some adolescents in this study specifically spoke of changing friends to a peer group more involved with sports as an alternative to drugs or substances generally. The following is illustrative:

I used to get high a lot . . . but then I started — like then I met Alfie. And he set a point, you know, he played football a lot. So I got into that. I've got into more athletics and stuff . . . I don't like to get high to do anything, like, I do sports or something to get high. [#134]

Q: If you knew about a community team, would you have gotten on it?

A: Yup.

Q: Do you think that would have helped you stay out of trouble?

A: Well, yeah. That uh, maybe, something to be responsible for, something to do. Keep you out of trouble. Just something to hold on to. [#138]

Others who did not use various substances associated athletes and athletics with nonuse of substances. These individuals spoke of the peers they currently had, peers who were athletes, and association with these peers as a reason for nonuse of substances. The following are representative excerpts:

Q: Do your friends smoke or drink?

A: No. They athletes too. Most everybody on street's athletes. They run track, cross-country, somethin' like that. [#138]

Q: You think that being interested in sports and being an athlete is part of what keeps you away from getting involved in stuff like that [drugs]?

A: Maybe, [heard stories about athletes who use drugs] but I don't think that anybody does. [#007]

For yet others, athletes themselves, involvement in sports was given as the reason for nonuse. The excerpts presented here are illustrative of sports specifically as a reason for nonuse or limited use of substances:

I don't do any drugs when I'm skating. That's like — that's my serious, you know, I won, money and stuff, you know, it's fun and stuff, I like it. And, you know, I don't mean to be conceited, but I'm good. You know. I don't, I don't do any kind of drugs at all when I'm skating. [#037]

[Some players] asked me if I wanted it [marijuana] and I said no. I figured if I was high I wouldn't know what I was doing and I was gonna line up against some pretty big players and I wanted to know what I was doing so if I ever got hurt or could've gotten hurt, I could've known what to do.

I think drugs are the worst thing. The way it messes up your body . . . I just couldn't do that to me, that's torturing me. [#029]

People who do sports are kinds of serious about it. If you're on the football (or the basketball) team, you don't smoke or don't do anything. . . . Marijuana, that can, you know, get you messed up too . . . people say it makes you feel good, if you just, if you're going to smoke it and just lie in your bed, you know, and just, I don't know, rest or something, go to sleep. But, uh, if you're out doing something (sports) and you get all high, then that's different cause you don't know what you're doing, you can't control yourself. [#019]

The excerpts presented in this section are indicative of an awareness on the part of some of the adolescents in this study of the peer group as a factor in their lives and as a factor in their drug use/nonuse. At the same time, these accounts also reveal an awareness on the part of these adolescents of the element of choice and rational decision making in their selection of peers and friends.

Further, the findings presented in this section seem to suggest some evidence that having or making friends active in sports (if not the individual's own actual participation in sports) is in fact a mechanism of "rehabilitation" elected by at least a few individuals in this study; that for others, sports peers or sports involvement is a mechanism of "prevention of drug use"; and that sport was one more type of peer group, which in this case seemed to discourage drug use.[21]

The Myth of Sports and "Clean Living": Sports and Substance Use/Nonuse

The youth in this study obviously live within the larger social world, a world which has held (perhaps until recently) a belief — perhaps a myth — that athletics and sports involvement go hand-in-hand with "clean living" (Rooney, 1984; Research & Forecasts, 1983). However, the findings of this study seem to indicate that the popular conception that sports and "clean living" go hand-in-hand, especially among youth, may indeed be a myth. Simply because an adolescent was an athlete did not mean that she/he did not use various drugs (including alcohol). Table 4.3 presents information concerning the extent of beer, liquor, and marijuana use, as revealed in the adolescents' own accounts, of those youth classified as participants in organized sports, as recreational athletes, and as nonathletes.

Table 4.3 shows that out of thirty-six youth involved in organized sport, 50 percent were users (occasional or regular) of beer, 28 percent were users (occasional or regular) of liquor, and 42 percent were users (occasional or regular) of marijuana.[22] This table also shows that out of twenty-four youth involved in recreational sports, 75 percent were users of beer, 63 percent were users of liquor, and 54 percent were users of marijuana. When the category of recreational athlete is added to that of the organized athlete, even more evidence presents itself to attest to the fact that sports and "clean living" is a myth, if "clean living" is interpreted to mean nonuse of alcohol and other drugs.

However, Table 4.3 also shows that out of thirty-nine nonparticipants in sports, 77 percent were users of beer, 69 percent were users of liquor,

Table 4.3
Reported Use of Beer, Liquor, and Marijuana by Type of Sports Participant

	BEER: Nonuse or tried	BEER: Occasional or Regular	LIQUOR: Nonuse or tried	LIQUOR: Occasional or Regular	MARIJUANA: Nonuse or tried	MARIJUANA: Occasional or Regular
ORGANIZED Sports Participants (N=36)	50%	50%	72%	28%	58%	42%
RECREATIONAL Sports Participants (N=24)	25%	75%	38%	63%	46%	54%
Nonparticipants in Sports (N=39)	23%	77%	31%	69%	31%	69%

NOTE: Total number of participants equals 99 because data are missing from one transcript.

and 69 percent were users of marijuana. This table shows that as the level of sports participation declines, regularity of use of all substances goes up, in all categories, pointing to a possible "temperance" effect of athletics.

The Myth of Sports and "Clean Living": "Jocks" and "Burnouts"

The data in the foregoing table show that the popular connection of sports and positive social behaviors such as absence of drug use appears to be a social myth. These data are indicators of actual behavioral practices as reported by the youth in this study. Related to this behavioral component is an attitudinal or belief component concerning the connection of sports and "clean living." It appears that this notion is not simply an abstract social myth characteristic of the larger world. The youth in this sample, despite their reported behaviors, also seem to accept the belief that sports and "clean living" go together.

For example, some of the adolescents make a distinction, stated or implied, between people they call "druggies" or "burnouts" and those they called "jocks." In a long response to a question about whether or not an individual liked school, one youth talked about the existence of two groups of people, by implication having different behaviors, a fact which he seemed to accept. He also then proceeded to define himself as still a different type of person, one who lived and acted in both worlds:

A: I don't like Oxford [school] thought. Because you, there's there's two kinds of people. There's either the burnouts or the preppies. And I'm neither one, I'm like in the middle.

Q: And what about the jocks?

A: They're preps. Yep. I was in with preps. And, you know I was, I'm like, a partying jock. You know I love sports. I'm athletic as hell but I like to party. [#037]

The distinction between drug use and sports is also made by some in response to questions about whom the adolescent thought used drugs. A typical response was, "Kids who are bad in school [use drugs]. Um, don't play no sports, uh, that's it" [#109]. Similarly, when asked why she was not involved in sports, another youth responded, "I hang out with people that are more, I guess, drug people" [#126].

Another youth also makes some similar distinctions, associates athletics with nonuse of substances and explains about his transition from being a "jock" to being a "druggie" and the effect that ultimately had on his athletic involvement:

> I was hanging out with a bunch of jocks. I was into sports and everyone was doing their homework first thing and then going and doing their sports. I had really good grades ... we used to play baseball ... beginning of junior high I was a jock. I used to hang out at [necs] and play basketball and stuff like that. Then when I was getting high I was still a jock, I'd still hang out but I'd get high too. After I started getting high, sports just sort of faded out of the picture, and the only thing I wanted to do is get high.[23] [#009]

However, not all of the youth, nor all of the youth who were athletes, maintained a separation of sports and substance use, either in belief or in behavior. Some athletes in fact talked about their use of various substances specifically in relation to athletic performance. For these individuals, use of codeine allowed one to play while injured, and use of marijuana and speed was seen to enhance performance (to be elaborated on in Chapter 5). Thus, for these individuals there existed an explicit and functional drug-sport connection (which was not seen by them as necessarily contradictory to the sports-"clean living" myth).

The foregoing emphasizes two facts: (1) that the notion of a marriage between sports and "clean living" (defined as the absence of drug use) is a popular societal myth, and (2) that it is also a myth held (revealed in direct statements about the distinction between "jocks" and "druggies") by the adolescents in this study. Athletes who were users of various substances seemingly had no problem (at least none about which they spoke) with the apparent contradiction between this myth and their sports participation and drug use. The one possible indicator of some type of awareness of possible contradiction (although not talked about as such) is the fact that, for some athletes, their substance use took place during their nonsport seasons and/or occasionally on the weekend, after the practices and game of the week were over. For example:

> Q: So you drank during the game season, sports seasons, but not as much?
>
> A: No, you know, this is like, you know, after the season was over.
>
> Q: How about when you're playin' on the basketball team, then?

A: Naw, you know, cause I, like drinkin', like you know, on the weekend, like when I'm at a party or somethin, you know, I'd have two or three beers.

Q: During the basketball season, you mean?

A: Ya, like, ah, on a weekend or something. [#135]

Sport-Drug Connection: General Beliefs

The youth also talked at length about their belief that, from their perceptions, there was another type of connection between drugs and sports: Specifically, athletes do use drugs, and that participation in athletics and drugs go hand in hand. For example, although he himself used no substances, one youth comments, "I find more athletes use it [drugs] than not athletes; the athletes get into it" [#029]. One of the most vivid examples of the sport-drug connection was in an extensive discussion by one male athlete concerning whether football players get high more often than basketball players, and why:

A: Pro basketball players were gettin' high, yup. I think it's pretty good. I'd like to see more players get high, and go out and play football . . . I think basketball players do it more cause there's more, there's more blacks in basketball than there is whites in football; but, um, they be, like, basketball players be gettin' high, snortin' all kinds of junk. Look at Richard Pryor; he got ripped.

Q: You don't think that's bad for them to be gettin' high all the time?

A: Naw, not really, they pro's.

Q: Do you think it makes them play better?

A: Yah.

Q: Why do you think everybody's making such a big deal about it then?

A: I dunno; they don't want them to do it. [#042]

These excerpts illustrate the fact that there coexist two very divergent views concerning the connection between drug use/nonuse and sports involvement. On the one hand, there is the popular conception that there is some connection between *nonuse* of drugs and involvement in sports. On the other hand, there also is the belief, reinforced by media coverage, that there is a definite connection between drug *use* and sports involvement. Within this sample this divergence is because different subjects who happened to be athletes held different views, and that some individuals managed to hold contradictory beliefs about the positive aspects of sports involvement *and* about the acceptability of substance use generally; and that others who held strong beliefs about sports also saw positive benefits in the use of specific drugs (e.g., speed) for purposes related to sports. That these very different views exist attests to the complexity of the issue of the sport-drug connections within society and within this sample of youth.

For some youth who have experience with athletic peers, beliefs which support the notion that athletics is a means by which to prevent or curtail drug use also support the social myth concerning the positive benefits of athletic participation. However, that some of the youth who express these beliefs concerning athletics and drug nonuse are involved in both sport *and* drug use attests to the discrepancy between that popular belief and their actual practices.

These disparate findings concerning sports and substance use also seem to support the notion that sports allow youth to form merely one more type of peer group that facilitates and encourages *or* discourages use of drugs. And more specifically, that rather than being deviant, drug usage is simply "a behavioral style which interrelates with interpersonal and socio-cultural factors" (Segal et al., 1980; Huba et al., 1979). That is, that drug use is in fact conforming, rather than deviant, behavior in some groups given the socio-cultural factors associated with adolescence and adolescent group activities.

SUMMARY

This chapter has presented information about the adolescents' social worlds, specifically the various activities in which the adolescents engage during their free time, with particular attention to the focal activity of concern to this study — sports participation/nonparticipation. This chapter has also discussed the broad issue of the place and meaning of sports in the lives of the athletically involved adolescents in this study, in relation to their life goals, their use of time, as a factor in liking school, and as a vehicle for interaction with and making new friends; also presented were the reasons why various youth were (or were not) involved in sports. Finally, information was presented about the popular myth that sports and "clean living" go hand-in-hand, especially among youth.

As was shown, sports participants and nonparticipants reported engaging in primarily the same activities, with the exception of sports; participation in sports was the major activity that distinguished participants from nonparticipants. The findings indicated that, for some of these youth, participation in sports was an important dimension of their social worlds, occupying their free time, serving as a life goal, and so on.

This chapter has also focused upon the general theme of the peer group as it related to the use and nonuse of the various substances (marijuana, alcohol, harder drugs) of concern in this study. In general, whether or not the individual was a participant or a nonparticipant in sports, users of various substances had friends who were users of the substance in question; nonusers had peers who were nonusers (Pisano and Rooney, 1988; Silverman, 1987; Adams and Resnik, 1985; American Association of School Administrators, 1985; Hawkins et al., 1985; Blount and Dembo, 1984; Rooney, 1982–83; Bonyun, 1981; Levine and Kozak, 1979; Seffrin and Seehafer, 1976; Montgomery County Drug Commission, 1971). In those cases where the individual did not use a substance but her/his peers did, the explanations from the respondent gave indications of a strong sense of self, of liking oneself the way one was. The accounts of some of the adolescents specifically addressed and elaborated upon a deliberate change in peer group, which coincided either with greater usage of a substance, or with curtailment of consumption.[24] Finally, the type of peer group most specifically identified in terms of a decision to cease or curtail substance use was a group whose members were involved with sports, which seems to support the idea of sports involvement as a peer group that discourages use of drugs.

However, given other findings presented in this chapter, it seems that the evidence for the question, "what part does the peer group play in an adolescent's social world, especially in relation to drug use/nonuse?" and, more particularly, "is sports involvement merely one more type of peer group which encourages or discourages use of drugs?" is quite mixed, at best. It does appear that for some individuals, sports involvement discourages substance use; for others, sports involvement may have no effect one way or another; for still other individuals, sports involvement may encourage specialized drug use (see Chapter 5).

Again, it must be recognized that there are not major differences in the activities of the social worlds of sports participants and nonparticipants, except for the fact that sports participants spend free time and time with friends playing sports. It appears that for most of the adolescents, sports and drugs are not mutually exclusive activities and that sports involvement and drug use are simply two of several activities that occupy an individual's free time and the time spent with her/his peers.

In relation to the popular myth of sports and "clean living," the findings revealed that there is both a behavioral component and an attitudinal or belief component related to the notion, both of which exist in the adolescents' worlds. As seen from the discussions of the youth in this study, the behavioral data strongly refute the notion that sports participation goes hand-in-hand with substance nonuse. In this sample, sports and substance use are apparently not mutually exclusive activities, since 60 percent of the youth who were athletes used beer, 42 percent used liquor, and 47 percent used marijuana. However, the findings also showed that a distinct belief system exists among the youth concerning the separation of drug use and sports involvement, a belief in the sports-"clean living" myth. The belief and the contradictory behavior reflect the myth and the reality of the larger social world. Thus, it seems that the notion of a marriage between sports and "clean living" (e.g., absence of drug use) is indeed but a myth, evident in the society at large and held by the adolescents in this study, despite reported behavior to the contrary.

At this point, the findings attest to the fact that there is *not* the separation of the two activities — substance use and sports involvement — that perhaps myth would have one believe. These findings are also further evidence that the differences between athletes and nonathletes may not be as pronounced as their similarities.

NOTES

1. The categories of participant and nonparticipant are derived from *all* the information contained in all the discussions of the adolescents, not merely from information given in response to these questions about use of free time. This is important to note, since not all those who are classified as sports participants indicated that participation in sports was something in which they engaged in their free time — this is especially true for the girls. In fact, many of the girls who were formerly involved in sports (classified as nonparticipants) gave as a reason for not continuing that sports took up too much of their time. Related to this, it could also be speculated that some girls did not consider the time spent in sports participation "free" time.

Reasons why some sports participants (females and males) did not mention their sports involvement as something done during "free" time can only be subject to speculation. Perhaps some of those involved in sports, both female and male, did not consider their participation as something that is done during "free" time, given the structure and commitment required by interscholastic sport.

2. This is not to say that sport was the only activity athletes mentioned doing in their free time, for they also mentioned many of the activities that nonathletes mentioned (see Tables 4.1, 4.2).

3.   Seventy-six percent of the adolescents, when former athletes are included, have at some point been involved in sports.

4.   In this study far more males than females are involved in both recreational (28% vs. 17%) and organized sports (42% vs. 25%). In contrast, Research & Forecasts (1983:33) indicates that 56 percent of the males and 49 percent of the females are "moderate" or recreational athletes; and 22 percent of the males and 14 percent of the females are "avid" or organized sports participants.

5.   Speculation can be offered here concerning the lack of available role models, opportunities to participate, and sport career options for women as compared to men.

6.   Often this notion of sport as a life goal was expressed in response to the question asking about the individual's goal in life, or to the question asking for the individual to project ten years into the future and describe what she/he would be doing. Sometimes this notion of sport as a life goal appeared as part of other types of discussions in which sports were a major topic.

7.   Of these with sport as a life goal, 50 percent were users of beer, 50 percent were users of liquor, 21 percent were users (only occasional) of marijuana; none used any hard drugs.

8.   Out of the total sample in this study, 27 percent are black or from racial minorities.

9.   Of these athletes who indicated that sports were a way in which they used their time, about 37 percent were users of beer (most only occasionally), 14 percent were occasional users of liquor, 29 percent were users of marijuana (regular), and one individual was an occasional user of speed.

10.   Another bit of evidence attesting to how much time sports consume is the fact that several nonathletes (female) who had previously been involved with organized sports gave as their reason for not continuing involvement the amount of time the sport took. For example: "And I don't know, this year, I didn't feel like it [being on softball team], there's a lot of other things going on . . . it's right after school you'd go out and do sports and I just, I would feel tied down, and I'd like to do whatever I want" [#141].

11.   Of the athletes, 38 percent mentioned the importance of sports and friends; of this 38 percent, 43 percent were users of beer (mostly occasionally), 17 percent were users of liquor (occasional), 26 percent were users of marijuana (almost all regular); there was only one individual who occasionally used speed.

12.   Although only one youth elaborated upon this particular theme (perhaps because he was the only one questioned specifically about it), such comments suggest that sports involvement might be a factor that provided a reason to remain in school for this youth and others like him.

13.   For sociologists (particularly sports sociologists and those interested in gender issues) and for physical educators, the fact that females primarily stated they found activity "boring and tiring" should suggest a need for research in this area.

14.   Of these eight youth who articulated that they found sports boring, four were regular users of beer; four were users of liquor (three regularly); three were regular users of marijuana; one was a regular user of speed; and one was a regular user of both acid and cocaine.

15.   Typically, given the cultural expectations that males and females receive in American society, gender role socialization may explain not only why girls may not be active in sports, especially as they move into and through high school, but also

some of the other activity differences mentioned earlier. These cultural expectations might also relate to what adolescent girls say they do, as opposed to what they may really do.

16. The movement from junior high school into and through senior high school may also account for the nonparticipation of other youth in sports. Junior high school sports are often not as highly competitive nor as highly selective so that there are not necessarily team "cuts" by virtue of which less-skilled players do not make the team. Similarly, junior high school sports sometimes (not always) may be specifically a mechanism by which all who wish to play are given that opportunity, and the focus may be on skill building rather than on competition. As one moves into the senior high school the number and variety of teams may increase, but at the same time the selectivity factor usually becomes greater because of the emphasis upon winning, allowing only the "best" to gain team membership. Thus, fewer individuals have an opportunity to play organized school-related sports (especially "major sports") as they progress from junior high to senior high school.

17. The question of causality is not one with which this study is concerned, even though much of the literature seems to be concerned with it. What is of concern here are the individual's own words and accounts, the youth's own reasons and explanations of substance usage, and the individual's references to her/his peers in that context.

18. Most juvenile delinquency literature also discusses activities, specifically delinquent activities, within the context of group membership (e.g., delinquent "gangs").

19. These aspects of the peer group theme are also touched upon in Chapter 5, in the section dealing with substance availability.

20. Since the number of regular users of hard drugs is so small (N = 10), that category is not included here.

21. On the other hand, since many athletes indicated that their friends (also athletes) used drugs, and since friends were often the source of the substances, this suggests evidence to the contrary: that sports involvement is simply one more type of peer group which may facilitate or encourage substance use.

22. Use of wine and hashish, as well as all harder drugs, has been left out of this table because the total number of users (defined as regular and/or occasional use) is so small (e.g., 21 users of wine, 20 users of hashish, 18 users of speed, 4 users of Quaaludes).

23. Apparently, for this particular subject, involvement in sports did not succeed as a means by which to prevent substance usage. His comment, however, implies that there is a *belief* that sports involvement and having friends who are involved in sports will act, and perhaps did act for a time, as an influence against substance use.

24. No attempt is made or intended at causal interpretation of these peer group changes. The accounts simply tell the story of peer group change coincident with *desire to curtail* or *actual curtailment* of substance use, or *desire to increase* or *actual increased* usage of the various substances.

5

Adolescents' Explanations for Use and Nonuse of Drugs

The preceding chapter discussed some of the similarities and differences between the social worlds of the adolescents in this study, with particular attention to sports participation. This chapter will deal primarily with the following questions: What are the explanations offered by adolescents regarding their use/nonuse of drugs? How do the explanations of drug use/nonuse offered by youth involved in sports compare with the explanations of drug use/nonuse by youth not involved in sports? The questions of whether involvement in sports is a mechanism of prevention of or rehabilitation from drug use and whether sports involvement is a "temperance" mechanism will also be briefly addressed. These last two issues were also addressed in the preceding chapter.

The subjects in this study have spoken at great length about their lives and their thoughts, explanations, perceptions, and activities related to various aspects of their lives, including extensive accounts and explanations of drug usage and nonusage. During the course of these discussions, various reasons were offered that explained both drug use and nonuse. These reasons and explanations will be presented here, with use of drugs dealt with first.

SUBSTANCE USE

This section presents a number of reasons why adolescents say they use alcohol and marijuana, and how they explain trying harder drugs. It must be noted that very few of the adolescents can be said to be regular, or even occasional, users of one or more hard drugs; yet many of the youth have tried a number of the drugs classified as hard drugs (mainly speed, cocaine, Valium; the current fads of crack and ice were unheard of at the time of the study and there was no mention of steroid use). Since the accounts and reasons of those adolescents who have tried various hard drugs parallel themes from the accounts of regular and occasional users of marijuana and alcohol, reasons given for use of all substances are included in this chapter.

As was shown in Chapter 4, the social worlds of the youth who participate in sports and those who do not are quite similar, except for participation in sports. Similarly, many of the reasons for use of alcohol, marijuana, and harder drugs that emerged from the youths' discussions are expected reasons (e.g., the thing to do at parties or concerts, peers' use, to get high or drunk), and basically show no particular patterns of difference between sports participants and nonparticipants (except as indicated in the previous chapter).

A variety of explanations emerged from the accounts of the youth concerning their substance usage. Some of these reasons are particular to only one type of substance; some, to two or three substances; and a few reasons apply to all of the various drug substances. It should also be noted that these reasons or explanations are not mutually exclusive. Often several reasons for use or nonuse were included in the adolescents' explanations. The variety of explanations can be subsumed under three larger themes that include: effects of the substance, "environmental" factors (e.g., availability and parties), and "motivational" reasons (e.g., no particular reason, boredom).

Effects of the Substance

The theme that encompassed the largest number of specific reasons was that concerning the effects of the substance. Four major categories are subsumed in this theme: physical effects, mental and emotional effects, specific effects — getting high or drunk, and specific effects — fun. Again, within this large theme, the specific reasons are not mutually exclusive. Each of these reasons will be presented with representative excerpts from the accounts of the adolescents.

Physical Effects. The physical effects of a substance as a reason for use was given for all three categories of substance: alcohol, marijuana, and hard drugs, primarily speed. Except as noted, there were no noticeable differences between athletes and nonathletes in the explanations given, nor between females and males. Included under the theme of physical effects for alcohol, for some youth, was the reason that they simply "liked the taste" or that it "quenched thirst":

I don't, I don't drink beer because it gets me loaded. I drink beer because I like the taste of it. [#101]

I drink liquor because it quenches my thirst. [#106]

The primary physical effect for which marijuana was used was to assist with sleep. This use of marijuana as a kind of sedative was expressed by a number of youth, and the marijuana was usually used for this purpose when the individual was alone, "When I did smoke alone, it was with the intention of helping me sleep" [#113].

For other marijuana users, when asked why they smoked, the reason for use was a type of physical effect that could be described as enhancement — giving more energy, making one less tired. This explanation was given basically by athletes:

I just feel loose. . . . Well, if I'm tired, or something, from then, before I smoke it, after I get finished, I don't feel tired that much. [#038]

I have more energy . . . I can concentrate more . . . I love playing sports when I'm high. Cause, I just go all out, you know. I don't, I don't get ridiculous, go all out, you know, so I could hurt myself, but, you know, I go all out, and just get into — I'm more uh, um, like I'm the one that's always yowling, saying come on, let's do this, let's do that, you know. [#037]

Speed was the most frequently used of the so-called harder drugs and its use was effect-specific: for energy or staying awake. Codeine was also used by athletes for a specific reason, namely to relieve pain. The following are typical comments concerning speed:

Speed . . . wakes you up . . . [I used] it once every two weeks, even when I was on track. Cause it helped me run. It kept me going' . . . I can run farther. [#033]

If I feel, you know, I feel like partyin', but I'm not really into it, I'll take a couple speeds and just keep going ya going, like if you're real beat after a long day or somethin' and you feel like going out partyin' but you just don't have the energy. There it is. [#124]

Mental and Emotional Effects. Users of marijuana more often indicated mental or emotional effects as a reason for their use of marijuana than did users of alcohol or harder drugs. These mental and emotional effects — specifically, mood alterations (e.g., to get in a "good mood," to get "mellow," or to "relax," etc.) — were the most prevalent and pronounced reasons for marijuana use. These findings parallel those found in a number of other studies (Segal, 1977; Shearn and Fitzgibbons, 1973). These mental and emotional explanations were given by both athletes and nonathletes, and were predominantly given by males in the 16- to 18-year-old age range. The following are typical representative excerpts:

It's a different feeling, a different change. From like being straight . . . [it] relaxes, jes feel relaxed. [#044]

Well, yea yea. Well, you want to get in like a good mood I get high. I get in a good mood. [#003]

Well, it just mellows me out. [#034]

In a similar fashion, users of alcohol (although not nearly so many as was the case with marijuana use), in response to questions about why they drank, also indicated mood alteration (e.g., "better mood," "makes me feel good") as a reason for their drinking (especially of beer). More females than males gave this particular reason for use of alcohol:

I drink because . . . it releases my inhibitions. [#116]

Um, I guess to get in a better mood. [#111]

Finally, as far as hard drugs were concerned, since there were so few users of hard drugs, there were even fewer individuals who gave specific reasons having to do with emotional effects for their use of these drugs. However, there were some individuals who expressed these emotional and mental reasons (e.g., makes me "mellow" or "relaxes" me) when asked questions about why they used drugs, specifically, acid, Valium, or cocaine: "Oh, they [drugs] were doing a lot, they were helping me a lot . . . I was more relaxed and, and easy-going. . . . [Valium] Because I was, as I told you in, last time, I was, I was depressed and I didn't feel good. . . . Stress especially. Stress, it was real hard" [#114].

Mental and emotional effects as a reason for use were given by more marijuana users than by the users of other substances. Of those explaining marijuana use in terms of getting "mellow" or because it "relaxed" the individual, 82 percent were female (60% of all female marijuana users),

18 percent were male (5% of all male marijuana users); 36 percent were athletes (14% of athletes who used marijuana), 63 percent were nonathletes (30% of all nonathletes who used marijuana).

Specific Effects: Getting High or Drunk. When asked why they used a particular substance, many of the adolescents gave as a reason simply "to get high" or "to get drunk"; this parallels the findings of Minatoya and Sedlacek (1979) and Brown and Finn (1982). Of the adolescents who gave "to get drunk" as a reason for alcohol use, 30 percent were athletes (17% of all athletes who used alcohol); 70 percent were nonathletes (47% of all nonathletes who used alcohol); of those who said they used marijuana "to get high," 55 percent were athletes (21% of all athletes who used marijuana), 45 percent were nonathletes (19% of all nonathletes who used marijuana). The majority giving this reason for use were 16 and 17 years of age. The following are excerpts representative of these types of comments, for marijuana and alcohol, respectively:

> I don't know, I just — it's something that I always want to do is get high. [#047]

> [I] do [drink to get drunk] because I have more fun when I'm drunk . . . I'm always comfortable. [#114]

In terms of harder drugs, when an individual was asked why she/he tried or used a given drug, "getting high" or "getting a buzz" was a reason specifically mentioned for both acid and cocaine (sometimes in terms of a preference for the particular drug over other substances precisely because of the perception of a "better high"). Of those who gave this reason, a much larger percentage of nonathletes (90%) than athletes (10%) explained their drug use and/or trial of hard drugs in these terms. For example, "Cause I thought it'd [acid] be a good buzz. . . . It's [cocaine] a real good buzz, I like the buzz" [#047].

Specific Effects: Fun. For some adolescents, the answer to queries about use of marijuana and alcohol was simply that it was "fun"; this parallels the findings of Seffrin and Seehafer (1976). It was sometimes also tied to the notion of getting high or drunk, with essentially no elaboration about what "fun" meant. Since respondents quite frequently offered "fun" as a reason by itself (that is, separate from the notion of getting drunk or high), it is maintained as a separate response category, in order to refrain from a researcher-imposed definition, as it appears to have some meaning to the respondents separate from getting high or drunk (even though they gave no exact definition of "fun"). Of those giving this explanation for marijuana use, 78 percent were male (17% of all male marijuana users), 22 percent were female (13% of all female marijuana users); of those giving this explanation for alcohol (beer) use, 63 percent were male (11% of all male alcohol users); 37 percent were female (15% of all female beer users). Likewise, of those giving "fun" as a reason for marijuana use, 44 percent were sports participants (14% of all athletes who used marijuana), 56 percent were nonathletes (19% of nonathletes who used marijuana). Of those giving this reason for alcohol (beer) consumption, 50 percent were athletes (11% of athletes who used alcohol), 50 percent were nonathletes (15% of nonathletes who used alcohol).

Situations that often were described as coinciding with the adolescents' descriptions of smoking or drinking because it was "fun" included the nonspecific (e.g., simply being with friends), as well as the specific (e.g., being at a party, attending a concert).[1] Sometimes, also, the individual gave no indication of any situational context and may have, in fact, indicated that friends were not a factor in the smoking or drinking. Some individuals did not expand upon their statements and simply stated something to the effect that they wanted to get high because "it's fun." In response to questions about why an individual smoked and/or drank, the following are typical responses expressing this reason:

Q: Were you with other people that were smoking or what?

A: I don't know. They smoked all the time, I didn't, so that didn't have nothing to do with it [smoking]. I just just, I don't know. I felt like getting high again. I want to get high because it's fun. [#003]

I don't know. Just had fun. [#030]

Q: How about, um, why do you drink in groups?

A: Um, it's funner to talk to someone else. I used to drink alone, when I used to drink a lot. [#143]

The foregoing reasons (physical effects, mental and emotional effects, specific effects — getting high or drunk, and specific effects — fun), within the broader theme of effects of the substance, account for the bulk of the reasons offered in response to various inquiries about why an individual used any of the various substances. There are a few other reasons that were given with some frequency by the adolescents, and these fall into the two remaining broad thematic categories: "environmental" factors (i.e., availability and parties) and "motivational" factors (i.e., for the sake of doing it, and to alleviate boredom).

"Environmental" Factors

Within this theme there are two types of "environmental" factors revealed in the accounts of the users, both of which have to do with availability of the substance: general availability, and specific availability — that is, environments such as parties. These environmental availability reasons for use of a substance were mentioned across all substances, but general availability was mentioned by many more individuals in regard to marijuana and hard drugs than for alcohol.[2] There were no particular distinctions between participants and nonparticipants in sports in terms of general availability.

Specific availability — that is, parties — was mentioned by more individuals in relation to alcohol than to any other substance. In total, of those giving the party explanation, 50 percent were female and 50 percent were male. Looking specifically at beer consumption, 50 percent of the female alcohol users compared to 20 percent of the male alcohol users gave "party" as the explanation; 22 percent of the athletes who used beer and 41 percent of the nonathletes who used beer gave this as a reason for their use.

General Availability. For many youth, availability of a substance was given as a reason to use the substance; often availability was simply expressed by saying the substance in question was "around."[3] The following is a typical response concerning marijuana: "I just decided I wanted to try it sometime, and then I just started to ... when it's around you smoke it" [#018].

Specific Availability: Parties. While the adolescents did not often mention general availability as a reason for alcohol use, when asked about reasons for use of alcoholic substances, the occasion of a party was frequently the response. The following excerpts are representative:

> I dunno, ... so that's it — a beer party, well I dunno, just a party, party, a regular party. [#035]

> I'm not a drinker. Every once in a while I'll go out to a party and I'll have a drink or something. [#012]

"Motivational" Reasons

Still other reasons were given for use, most predominantly for the use of harder drugs. These could be called "motivational" reasons and fell into the category of simply wanting to try or have the substance (whatever it was), or using the substance because it was "something to do" or because the individual was bored.

For the Sake of Doing It. Most of the youth did not elaborate upon this reason; they simply stated this reason when asked about their use of some drug. This response was given in reference to a number of different harder drugs, with Valium, cocaine, and acid being the drugs most frequently mentioned in this context. For example:

[Valium] . . . just a regular day, no particular reason. [#047]

[Speed] I just do it for the hell of it, I guess. [#032]

Boredom or Something to Do. The other type of "motivational" reason given for use of a substance was because use was "something to do" and/or because the individual was bored. This finding coincides with much research (Adams and Resnik, 1985; Wasson, 1981; Minatoya and Sedlacek, 1979; Butler, 1976; O'Connor, 1976; Guinn, 1975; Messolonghites, 1974; Samuels and Samuels, 1974; Cohen, 1973; Spady, 1971; Clinard and Wade, 1966; Briar and Piliavin, 1965; Bordua, 1960; Schafer, 1969a, 1969b), which has reported that "delinquency" in various forms results from sheer boredom. The explanation of boredom was given mainly in response to questions about alcohol use. Of those giving "boredom" as a reason for alcohol use, 66 percent were male (16% of all male alcohol users), 33 percent were female (30% of all female alcohol users); 56 percent were athletes (22% of all athlete alcohol users); 44 percent were nonathletes (30% of all nonathlete alcohol users). Most of those giving boredom as a reason for use of various substances were between 14 and 15 years of age. The following are illustrative excerpts:

It was just, I dunno, it was really we just had nothin' to do, so. [#043]

Sometimes when I'm by myself, I drink a beer. I get kind of tired and bored. . . . You know, I be bored and I have nothing else to do, just drink a little bit of beer, put the rest aside. [#039]

The foregoing sections have presented the various explanations the youth offered as reasons for their drug use; these reasons included some specific substance effects, and some "environmental" and "motivational" factors pertaining to drug use. Most of the reasons and explanations discussed above were offered by both males and females (see Table 5.1) and by both participants and nonparticipants in sports (see Table 5.2). Thus, in relation to the question of how the explanations of drug use offered by youth involved in sports compare with those of youth not involved, there were no major differences, except that a notably larger percentage of nonathletes drank to get drunk and drank because alcohol was available. Yet there were some different explanations offered only by sports participants; the following section, in contrast, will present these explanations offered by sports participants, which were explanations in which involvement in sports was connected to their use of various drugs.

Sports and Substance Use

In general, in terms of discussion about substance use and substance use and sports, athletes did not appear markedly different from nonathletes as far as reasons for use of substances was concerned (nonuse will be dealt with in the next section). Nonetheless, there was one reason for use which athletes revealed that nonathletes did not. Athletes who used marijuana gave a reason related to sports

Table 5.1
Reasons for Use of Alcohol and Marijuana Mentioned by at Least 20 Percent of Female and Male Users of Alcohol and/or Marijuana

Reason	Females	Males
	N = 20*	N = 46*
Boredom	30%	26%
Get Drunk (Alcohol)	45%	24%
Get High (Marijuana)	**	24%
Get Mellow (Marijuana)	45%	***
Party (Alcohol)	50%	20%

*Includes regular and occasional users of beer, liquor, or marijuana.
**Mentioned by less than 20 percent of female users.
***Mentioned by less than 20 percent of male users.

Table 5.2
Reasons for Use of Alcohol and Marijuana Mentioned by at
Least 20 Percent of Athletes/Nonathletes Who Used
Alcohol and/or Marijuana

Reason	Athletes	Nonathletes
	N = 36*	N = 30*
Party (Alcohol)	22%	41%
Get Drunk (Alcohol)	**	47%
Boredom	22%	27%
Get Mellow (Marijuana)	**	23%

*Includes occasional and regular users of alcohol and/or marijuana.
**Mentioned by less than 20 percent of the athlete users.

performance.[4] It was their belief that being high while engaged in sports enhanced performance in some way or another; this parallels the findings of Baugh (1970). Some of the athletes were also emphatic in their statements concerning their preference of marijuana over alcohol for sports performance and/or the use of marijuana for specific sports but not for others. The following are typical excerpts:

Depends on the mood I'm in. You know, if I want to play basketball, I'm not going to party. Or we'll [friends] get together and lift weights or something. And we do party when we lift, lift them. Not drinking, but smoking helps, motivate or something. [#143]

I love playing sports when I'm high. Cause I just go all out. You know, I don't, I don't get ridiculous, go all out, you know, so I could hurt myself, but you know, I go all out, and just get into — I'm more, uh, um, like I'm more — like if we're playing football, I'm the one that's always yowling, saying, come on, let's do this, let's do that, you know. . . . I have more energy, I can concentrate more. [#037]

While athletes used marijuana for sport-specific reasons, this was not the only substantive use for marijuana indicated by either athletes or non-athletes. For example, other substantive uses of marijuana included use as a sleeping aid and for mood alteration (as was seen earlier in this section). However, once again, it was only the athletes who indicated use of marijuana in direct connection with sports involvement and performance.

Although marijuana was the drug most frequently indicated as being used, two of the harder drugs were also used by a few of the athletes for specific purposes in relation to sports performance. These drugs included the amphetamine speed and the narcotic codeine. The following is a typical remark concerning speed:

> I used speed before a football game and I didn't want to stop running, you know, like in, the first, after the down, right, I sit there and had to, you know, jog by myself and, what, what's wrong, you know, said, I'm anxious to go man, got the ball I was like wow, what am I going to do with it, and I think. But I did all right for the game. [#036]

Several of the athletes had also indicated that in the past they had taken codeine in order to be able to continue playing while injured; one also indicated that he would do so in the future if he should become injured.[5]

Thus this section has presented findings which attest to the fact that there are differences between athletes and nonathletes in at least some of the explanations given for drug use. In addition, it appears that sport for some, rather than being a mechanism for prevention, rehabilitation, or temperance as mentioned in Chapter 4, may be the very reason for use of certain drugs.

Summary: Substance Use

This section has presented a number of reasons why adolescents do use alcohol and marijuana, and why they try harder drugs. These reasons, which emerged from the accounts of the youths themselves concerning their substance usage, were subsumed under three larger themes that included: effects of the substance, "environmental" factors (i.e., availability and parties), and "motivational" reasons (i.e., for the sake of doing it, and boredom). The specific reasons included in the broader thematic area of effects of the substance (i.e., physical effects, mental and emotional effects, getting high or drunk, and "for fun") were most frequently mentioned for the regular and occasional use of alcohol and marijuana, and for trying harder drugs.

The most frequently given reasons for alcohol use included getting drunk or buzzed, being at a party, being bored, and doing it for something to do. The most frequently mentioned reasons for the use of marijuana included mood alteration (getting mellow or relaxed) and simply because it was available. Attempting to summarize the reasons for trying harder drugs is a bit more complicated; some of the reasons were quite drug specific (e.g., using or trying speed to keep awake or for more energy; using or trying cocaine, Valium, or acid to relax). Other reasons were not limited to specific drugs: just to have, try, or do a substance and "because it was available" were reasons given for trying or using a variety of the harder drugs. Finally, there were so few users of hard drugs that summarizing reasons beyond the above is not practical. As was indicated, the explanations given by participants in sports and nonparticipants were not appreciably different, with the exceptions mentioned earlier concerning the sport-specific uses of marijuana, speed, and codeine, and the fact that a much greater percentage of nonathletes (47%) compared to athletes (17%) drink to get drunk.

Although many of the reasons for use that emerged from the youths' discussions are familiar reasons (e.g., parties, to get high or drunk), the findings may be important in that the themes emerge from the adolescents' own discussions, rather than from forced-choice questionnaires, and the data are presented, as far as possible, in the words of the adolescents themselves.

SUBSTANCE NONUSE: EXPLANATIONS OF FEAR

Regardless of whether individuals were participants in sports or not, and regardless of the type of substance in question, one common and pervasive theme related to limited use (i.e., having tried a substance) or nonuse of drugs was that of fear of the effects of a particular drug or drugs. The notion of fear as expressed by these individuals has two meanings, one of which could be called a "generalized" fear and the other of which could be called "fear of harming the body." The subjects' ability to articulate these fears ranged from the very vague to the quite specific, from simply being "scared" to fear of becoming "addicted." For some subjects, their perception of fear was a reason they did not use a particular substance; for other subjects, their fears served to limit the amount of a substance used.

Cannabis Substances

Cannabis substances, specifically marijuana, have been used, or at least tried, by 71 percent of the adolescents in this study. Marijuana (pot) is the most frequently used of these substances, since hashish and related products are, according to the subjects, more expensive and much less accessible than marijuana.[6] Despite the fact that many of these adolescents have tried or use cannabis substances on a limited basis, the mention of various kinds of fear is part of their discussions regarding limiting cannabis use and avoiding its use.

Generalized Fear. Each of the following explanations is representative of others like them. Each also is typical of the fact that, for some subjects, the fears that they talk about are unsubstantiated — that is, the fear has not been experienced in real life by themselves or their friends. For others, the fears about which they talk are substantiated — that is, they themselves, or friends of theirs, have experienced the feelings or effects of which the subject is now afraid.

Typical of the generalized fear and of the somewhat vague comments is the following:

A: One time [had a chance to smoke pot] with my friend, Ivan, he had some. And he asked me, did I want any. And I said no . . . 'cause I didn't want none. I was scared.

Q: What makes you scared?

A: I don't know.

Q: Do you think it can hurt you?

A: Yep.

Q: Did it seem to hurt [Ivan]?

A: Nope.

Q: Then why were you still scared?

A: I don't know. I wasn't going to take nothing. [#040]

A similarly general fear is expressed in the following:

Q: Do you still smoke pot or not at all?

A: Never. Don't touch it.

Q: How come?

A: Um, I just when I get high it's terrible. I just, I don't like the reaction. [#101]

The foregoing excerpts typify the unsubstantiated (the first exchange) and substantiated (second exchange) fears expressed by some of the youth.[7] Most of these explanations were given by 14- and 15-year-olds; likewise, of those who indicated generalized fear as a reason for nonuse of marijuana, 68 percent were sports participants (53% of all athletes who did not use marijuana), 32 percent were nonparticipants in sport (67% of all nonathletes who did not use marijuana).

Fear of Harming the Body. In contrast to these generalized fears, physical fears were mentioned specifically by sports participants, and included statements like the following:

Probably get cancer off it. [#032]

Yea, I quit . . . about, I don't know, eight months ago or so. It started to get to the point where like all the involuntary muscles in my heart, my heart, my lungs, and things like that, that you don't have to worry about normally, I had to worry about. I'd be sitting there, and you know, listening to music or talking to somebody, or listening, or whatever and all of a sudden my chest would start hurting, and I would realize that I hadn't been breathing for minutes at a time and I had to consciously make my heart work. And I was, it started to scare me, cause it started to happen a lot, and you know, and it was hurting bad. And so I quit. And I've been afraid to ever since. [#116]

These representative comments were from older adolescents (18 years of age), one of whom was a regular marijuana smoker, the other of whom had been a regular user but quit, specifically because of the physical effects and fears. Representative comments from younger adolescents (13 and 14), neither of whom had even tried marijuana, reflected physical fears of a more diffuse, nonspecific nature, perhaps because of their limited experience and exposure to marijuana:

A: Marijuana's harmful.

Q: And what does marijuana do, and other drugs?

A: Well, they don't even know what it does. They already have a list of harms, and they're trying to list more, they don't even know. [#015]

A: [Kids] pass around a joint and offer me it, I've never really tried it. I always pass it down. I don't think it's good for your body or anything. [#014]

Fear of Addiction. A more specific fear, in which substances were seen as harmful both mentally and physically, was a fear of addiction, as witnessed in the following comments:

'Cause to me it's [pot] stupid, that's why I quit. . . . All it does is, you get hooked on it like cigarettes, drinking. Your body gets adjusted to it, and then you go crazy if you don't get it. [#031]

I don't think it's [pot] good for you. I don't know — that's the worst. I heard you can get addicted . . . I got it [the idea] from my health book. [#026]

Q: What do you think about marijuana?

A: Um, I don't know . . . marijuana don't do nothin' to ya . . . I don't know. I just, just like, I don't want ta get hooked on it, and I just don't feel like trying it right now. [#023]

This particular fear of addiction was mentioned primarily by younger (15 years of age or younger) adolescents who were non- or limited users of cannibis products. As seen above, this particular fear was the reason for quitting marijuana use by the oldest of these three subjects quoted. Fear of addiction was mentioned by about equal percentages of sports nonparticipants and participants. However, of the sports participants, all were participants in organized sports.

In summary, fear is a clear and pervasive explanation for nonuse, limitation of use, or curtailment of use of cannabis substances, especially marijuana. This category of explanation was mentioned by both males and females, participants and nonparticipants in sports, although fear of harming the body was more predominant among sports participants.

Alcohol

As was the case with marijuana, beer had been used, or at least tried, by 79 percent of the adolescents in this study; liquor had been tried, or used, by nearly as many of the youth; this parallels the findings of Baugh (1970). The discussions and explanations for the nonuse of the various alcoholic substances are quite similar. This section deals with fear as one major type of explanation, given primarily for nonuse of various types of alcohol, and occasionally for curtailment and/or cessation of alcohol use.

Of all the subjects in the study, about 33 percent were classified as non- or limited drinkers of beer (i.e., they had only tried or had never used or tried beer) and about 47 percent as nonusers of liquor (i.e., they had only tried or had never used nor tried liquor). Out of the accounts of these nondrinkers or limited drinkers, three fear-related themes emerged that explained the limited use and nonuse of alcohol. These themes parallel those that emerged related to marijuana, in that they include generalized fear, fear of harming the body, and fear of addiction. A fourth type of explanation was also present, and this was a dislike of the taste of the substance.

Generalized Fear: Loss of Control. An example of a generalized fear was fear of "loss of control." This was a concern and explanation mentioned by equal numbers of both males and females, blacks and whites, and by individuals who were sports participants and those who were nonparticipants in sports. Typical are the following:

> All beers taste really bad to me, except Michelob, I kind of like that a little . . . I don't really think there's anything wrong with it [drinking], unless you can't control yourself. Like if you do it too much, too often, and then you just go up to a point where you can't even help it. [#019]

> I think if you know how to control yourself, I mean if you don't drink it all the time. If you know how to control yourself like I know some people who drink every week. You know, a lot of beer and stuff like that. I don't think that's good. Especially because we're under age. Because they don't have control of themselves to drink that much. It [being in control] is very important to me. I don't want to be [??] and if I don't have control I don't know what I would do. So, I have complete control over myself. [#010]

Non- or limited drinkers of liquor gave similar fear-based explanations for their nonuse of liquor, as can be seen in the following accounts:

> *A:* I like drinkin' beer instead of wine or liquor.
>
> *Q:* Why?
>
> *A:* 'Cause liquor, you just go crazy when you drink that stuff, you get all hot. [#041]

Um, hard liquor, I just don't like it because I just, you know, I just imagine myself having a drink or two and then ending up and suddenly being on the floor. [#101]

Effects on the Body: General. Fear about effects on the body from alcohol use was expressed by some of the youth, most frequently by younger individuals (14- and 15-year-olds) involved in organized sports who were nonusers of liquor. Typical responses to the inquiry "Do you have some reasons for not drinking?" follow:

'Cause, alcohol is acid, ya know, and acid eats up your insides. [#023]

I just try to keep my body in good shape and stay from the things that will harm my body, like if I drink, like alcoholism. [#014]

In response to the same question, typical of limited users of liquor, is the following reason for limited use of liquor (and usually a preference for beer): "Liquor makes me all, all, buzzed out and mellow, well, you know, sloppy, falling down and shit, you know, I'd rather not be that way" [#117].

Fear of Harming the Body: Getting Sick. Another aspect of the fear of harming the body is the specific physical fear of getting sick. This reason for nonuse and/or curtailment of beer consumption was mentioned only by the sports participants who were nondrinkers or only occasional drinkers of beer. The following is a typical explanation:

I used to drink a whole beer by myself but I can't do it. I can't even drink a half . . . I had a spinning head, and sick to the stomach and I don't want to do that anymore . . . I don't drink at all at parties. I think I don't want because it gets you, um, hot and it makes you sick and I don't like it so I won't drink at parties. [#039]

Fear of getting sick was also a reason for limited use of liquor given by nonusers of liquor. Again, it was mainly the sports participants who expressed this particular fear as a possible result of liquor consumption. The following are representative explanations:

Q: You have any reason for not drinking?

A: Um um. Well, yeah, one time when I was over my friend's house one time — and he went into his father's bar. One time. And he brought a whole bunch of liquor and stuff, and we, drunk up all two bottles. And I got sick and I slept over at his house. [#040]

Q: Do you think you might ever try drinking again [after tasting scotch]?

A: No, 'cause I think I keep on hurtin' my stomach and I'll never forget, you know, that I got sick, you know, got sick. So, if I do it now, I think I'll just get sick again. [#025]

As was true of the accounts and reasons related to generalized fear regarding use of marijuana, accounts concerning the fear of getting sick fell into the two categories of unsubstantiated — that is, the fear had not been experienced in real life by themselves or their friends — or substantiated — that is, the respondents themselves, or friends of theirs, had experienced the feelings about which the subject expressed concern.

Fear of Addiction. As was the case with reasons for the nonuse of marijuana, fear of addiction, which can be seen as a fear with both mental and physical components, was a reason for nonuse of alcohol. Although fear of alcohol addiction was mentioned by only two adolescents, one of whom was a participant in organized sports and one of whom was not (and who occasionally drank), it may represent an important type of concern, since fear of addiction was mentioned in relation to other substances. The following are typical comments specifically pertaining to alcohol addiction, but the essence of which is similar to statements of fear of addiction to other substances:

Q: Do you have reasons for not drinking?

A: 'Cause . . . I ain't gonna get hooked on it. [#023]

I'm not a drinker. Every once in a while I'll go out to a party and I'll have a drink or something — you know, alcohol is not a big issue with me. . . . Alcohol is not a drug. It's a disease because you can get hooked on alcohol a lot easier than you can get hooked on anything else. [#012]

Dislike of Taste. The explanation for nonuse of alcohol given most frequently was that the individual did not like the taste of the substance. This explanation was mentioned basically by 14- to 16-year-olds, 26 percent of the nondrinking males and 79 percent of the nondrinking females, and 44 percent of the nondrinking athletes and 62 percent of the nondrinking nonathletes.[8] The following are typical statements:

Yeah, I don't like it. Never liked how it tasted or anything, and I just didn't really want to get into it. [#006]

Q: Do you drink beer?

A: No. It tastes nasty. [#038]

In sum, similar to the explanations for marijuana nonuse and curtailment, some comparable fear-related explanations were found in the respondents' accounts of alcohol nonuse. Generalized fears, as well as specific fears concerning harming the body, were mentioned as reasons for nonuse of both substances. Fear of getting sick from beer and liquor consumption was mentioned by participants in sports. Dislike of the taste of the substance was a frequently given explanation for nonuse of alcohol (and, as has been noted, some users of alcohol also indicated a dislike for the taste).[9,10] These were the most frequent explanations for alcohol nonuse, and there were not differences between sports participants and nonparticipants.

Hard Drugs

In contrast to beer, liquor, and marijuana, which were used by 66 percent, 52 percent, and 55 percent, respectively, of the adolescents in this study, only 27 percent of the youth reported using one or more of the harder drugs (i.e., speed, acid, cocaine, angel dust, heroin, Quaaludes, Valium, etc.), either occasionally or regularly. Those who had never used any of the harder drugs amounted to 43 percent of the adolescents. Of the adolescents who had tried any of the harder drugs, many had done so only once or twice; the most frequently tried drugs include speed, acid, and cocaine, with cocaine being the most frequently tried of the harder drugs. Of those who claimed they had tried speed (N = 28), 46 percent were athletes (22% of all athletes), 54 percent were nonathletes (38% of all nonathletes); of those who claimed they had tried acid (N = 24), 58 percent were athletes (23% of all athletes), 42 percent were nonathletes (25% of all nonathletes); of those who claimed they had tried cocaine (N = 31), 52 percent were athletes (27% of all athletes), 48 percent were nonathletes (38% of all nonathletes); of those who claimed to have tried Valium (N = 26), 46 percent were athletes (20% of all athletes), 54 percent were nonathletes (35% of all nonathletes); of those who claimed to have tried Quaaludes (N = 19), 47 percent were athletes (15% of all athletes), 53 percent were nonathletes (25% of all nonathletes); of those who claimed to have tried PCP (N = 11), 36 percent were athletes (7% of all athletes), 64 percent were nonathletes (18% of all nonathletes). Of those who had never used hard drugs, 73 percent were sports participants (and 71% of these were organized sports participants).[11]

From the accounts of nonusers of hard drugs, three fear-related themes emerged that explained their nonuse (i.e., either never having tried or having experimented only once or twice) of these substances. These themes parallel the themes found in the accounts of marijuana and alcohol nonuse, in that they include the categories of generalized fear, fear of harming the body, and fear of addiction.

Generalized Fear: Freakin' Out, Gettin' Messed Up. In the case of harder drugs, some of the accounts of the adolescents contained explanations of nonuse supported by fears that can be called generalized fears. Within this general category a dichotomy emerged, either the generalized fear was substance-specific, mainly in reference to angel dust, or the fear was generalized to all hard drugs. These explanations were given more often by 14- to 16-year-olds, by both males and females, athletes and nonathletes. The following quotes are illustrative of the substance-specific fear, the first two of angel dust and the last of cocaine:

Q: Would you use angel dust if a friend offered it to you?

A: Nope, from what I hear, that stuff is pretty potent, you can freak out on that stuff, I don't get into freakin' out. [#020]

Q: Angel dust?

A: No, not that. I heard too much shit about that stuff. It makes you crazy, kill yourself. [#035]

Q: What about cocaine?

A: I saw all the dangers of that stuff, so I said no — sometimes it could kill you. [#032]

The following are representative of reasons that have to do more with substance-generalized fear. These explanations came from all ages from 12 to 18, males and females:

Q: Can you tell me what your reasons are for not using any drugs?

A: Well, from drugs, like, you know, the hash and angel dust and LSD and heroin and codeine and all that, all the serious stuff. You know, the real junk that can really get you really messed up. [#019]

Q: Do you have serious reasons [for not using drugs]?

A: My own feelings are that, I guess, you know, the film strips and slides show that, you know, what they can do to you and I guess, in simulated, and how it can affect your perspective of life, and your perspective of something like a car coming toward you, and, um, this kind of scared the hell out of me, what it can do to you. [#017]

Q: Have you ever had a chance to take anything else [after trying speed]?

A: No, I didn't wanna take anything else, 'cause I didn't want, ya know. I been hearing things about people getting high off of pills, and I was kind of scared when I took speed. [#039]

The above excerpts are representative of the reasons categorized as generalized fear, a fear of "freakin' out" or "getting messed up," and being scared. These reasons were given for nondrug use by the majority of the adolescents.

Fear of Harming the Body. In contrast to general fears, such as being "scared" and "getting messed up," the adolescents expressed some specifically physical reasons for not using drugs, including the fear of death. Like the generalized-fear explanations, these were given by all ages from 13 to 20, males and females, athletes and nonathletes. The following are typical reasons for nonuse of hard drugs, each of which is in response to the question, "Do you have reasons for not using drugs?"

Yeah, well they, they do a lot of harm to your organs, first of all, and second of all, they're not really necessary. They don't, you know, taste good or anything like that. [#015]

My body just doesn't take in something like that. I think that might be the kinda thing that happens to a lot of people. I think my body would react bad to drugs. [#014]

I think drugs are the worst thing. The way it messes up your body. [#029]

Those things can kill! [#016]

Some of the youth, almost all males and a disproportionate number of blacks between the ages of 14 and 16, specifically mentioned a fear of death from drugs as a reason for their nonuse.

Q: Did you use some [drugs]?

A: Nope ... I was scared of it.

Q: Why?

A: 'Cause, all these drug pictures. They show, people die off of it. [#040]

Q: Do you think you will ever use drugs?

A: No. I can sit here and tell you a thousand times, you know, but I just can't see myself lowering, ya know, get lowered down to that standpoint, using drugs, ya know.

Q: Why do you think it's lowering?

A: Why? Just something proven to me. I don't want to die. It doesn't do anything to me but worry me. [#022]

These physical reasons for nonuse of drugs were mentioned, in some form or other, by nearly all of the nonusers of hard drugs; 61 percent of those who gave physical reasons were sports participants (23% of all sports participants), 39 percent were nonparticipants (23% of all nonparticipants in sport).

Fear of Addiction. As was the case with reasons for the nonuse of both marijuana and alcohol, fear of addiction (e.g., "getting hooked"), which can be seen as a fear with both mental and physical components, was a reason for nonuse of hard drugs. This fear was expressed by individuals of all ages, male and female, athlete and nonathlete. The following are typical explanations:

Q: Do you have some reason for not using drugs?

A: I just don't want to get hooked on that stuff or get stronger dependence. It makes your body want it more after you've had it a few times ... I don't want to get hooked on any of those [hard drugs]. [#027]

Q: Do you have some reason for not using drugs?

A: We studied it in school. And, you know, they can be addicting real fast, and then they tell us about the withdrawal symptoms, get sick, and, I just don't want to go through that. [#013]

I don't know, 'cause people that be hooked into it and they can't get it. You go crazy and stuff. [#107]

Q: What's your worst fear? What's the thing you fear most that would happen if you tried one of these other drugs like cocaine or LSD or one of these pills?

A: Getting addicted to it. . . . I couldn't see myself with those things.

Q: So you are only afraid of getting addicted and having to use it? You're not worried about going crazy or any weird things?

A: Well I'm worried about that too. But that's after I get addicted to it. [#110]

Each of these explanations for nonuse of hard drugs illustrates that in terms of hard drugs, for most of the subjects, the fears they give as reasons for nonuse of drugs are unsubstantiated — that is, the sensations and experiences about which they are afraid and of which they speak have not been experienced in real life by themselves or their friends. In fact, some of the adolescents indicated that what they have learned (i.e., the fears they have acquired), they obtained from movies on TV and from movies, textbooks, and outside speakers in their health classes. For example, the following were given in response to questions about why she/he felt the way she/he did about drugs:

Because I see it on TV, the people take drugs . . . in movies. [#107]

I got it [the idea of addiction] from health book. Yeah, well, you know, they talk about it a lot in health.[12] [#026]

In sum, the fear-related explanation was found in the majority of the nonusers' accounts regarding hard drugs. Fear of physical harm was mentioned consistently in regard to all types of drugs by participants in sports. Some nonparticipants in sports mentioned this fear of physical harm, but these were few in number and more often specific to a given category of drugs.

No regular users of hard drugs mentioned any general fear (i.e., those effects portrayed in media images — for example, "going crazy" or addiction) of doing harm to themselves mentally or physically, nor did they mention any fear of addiction in their accounts of drug use. However, some of them did express concerns about their drugs being tampered with in some fashion (e.g., marijuana laced with angel dust, cocaine being cut with sugar).[13]

As was seen above, the majority of adolescents who expressed a fear of addiction as a reason for nonuse of substances, especially of hard drugs, were sports participants. In fact, of these all were participants in organized sports. Sports involvement per se seems also to be a reason for the nonuse of most hard drugs, as well as other substances, as the following section will explain.

SUBSTANCE NONUSE

Non-Fear Explanations

While the above explanations related to the various types of fears were the most frequently mentioned and the most well-articulated of the explanations for nonuse of the various substances, there were several other types of explanations. These included the illegality or "wrongness" of substance use, having no opportunity to try various substances, having no desire to use various substances, and involvement in sports.

The notion of illegality or wrongness was a reason offered for nonuse of all the various substances (alcohol, marijuana, hard drugs); of individuals mentioning this, 71 percent were sports participants (20% of all athletes) and 15 years old was the modal age of these respondents. Their abilities to elaborate and offer accompanying explanations varied by substance. With marijuana, the notion of illegality or wrongness was often accompanied by the notion of "getting busted" or put in jail. For example:

> *A:* I don't want to get involved with it [pot smoking]. I just don't want to get involved with this, with something like that.
>
> *Q:* Why do you feel that way?
>
> *A:* 'Cause, um, you can get into a lot of trouble . . . police officers can — you get put in jail. [#025]

With alcohol, the explanations indicated a notion that there was an age ("older," "more than fifteen") when it was not wrong to drink:

> I don't think it's right for somebody, ya know, for somebody our age . . . I've always thought of it as something you are supposed to do when you are older. That you can do. That's how I feel. [#026]

I don't think there's anything wrong unless you're young, less than fifteen. [#019]

In terms of harder drugs, if adolescents even indicated any notion of illegality or wrongness, they were often unable or unwilling to elaborate upon their feelings.

No opportunity (i.e., they were not friends or acquaintances with people who used and/or supplied drugs; they were not in places where substances were used) to use substances was a reason given by many of the respondents; of these, 69 percent were sports participants (18% of all sports participants) and 15 years old was the age of most of these respondents. However, the predominance of the responses varied according to the particular substance, with more of the youth indicating no opportunity to use hard drugs (sometimes this was substance specific) and somewhat fewer indicating no opportunity to use marijuana. *There was not a single adolescent who indicated no opportunity to use alcoholic substances.* This latter fact is evidence of similarity in the social worlds of the adolescents in this study — regardless of age, sex, or participation/nonparticipation in sports — and is an issue to be particularly noted, not only in terms of policy development but also within the context of understanding the larger society and culture of which these adolescents are a part. If notice is not taken of the fact that all adolescents had the opportunity to use alcohol, understanding of the processes of alcohol use and attempts to develop meaningful policy will neglect to focus upon what is probably a critical factor — that is, opportunity for alcohol use across types of groups to which adolescents belong.

No desire was the overwhelming non-fear explanation for the nonuse of the various substances. Few adolescents indicated no desire to try alcoholic substances. Most of the youth who indicated no desire to try marijuana or hard drugs were individuals who had never tried either substance. Sometimes the explanation of lack of desire was elaborated upon, but most often it was not. Of those indicating no desire to try the various substances, 71 percent were sports participants (36% of all sports participants).[14]

Sport and Substance Nonuse

Although it is the case that sports and substance use are not generally mutually exclusive activities for some athletes, sports involvement and/or affiliation with athletes, however, can be a means to an end — that end being nonuse of drugs. However, sports involvement as a reason for nonuse is complicated. That is, some individuals report either (1) that they will not use certain substances because of their sports involvement at the same time as their accounts indicate that their sports involvement has no effect upon the use of other substances; or (2) that they will not use certain substances because of their sports involvement at the same time as they indicate that they do use certain other substances because of the perceived positive effects of that substance upon their sports involvement or performance. Still, for yet other participants in sport, involvement is a definite and unqualified reason not to use any substances. It must be kept in mind that these explanations are characteristic almost solely of the male sports participants in this study. The female sports participants are fewer in number and they spoke less about their sports involvement; only one made any comment about sports and its relations to drug use/nonuse.

With this sex distinction in mind, then, sports involvement and/or affiliation with athletes may serve as a means of prevention and/or rehabilitation from drug use for some individuals; second, athletic involvement may be a mechanism for "temperance" of drug usage for some individuals. Both the goal of "temperance" and the "influence against use of drugs" of sports involvement is dealt with next (and was touched upon in the previous chapter in relation to the sports peer group).

Temperance. Involvement in sports was, for adolescents so involved, a reason given for their limiting substance use, specifically alcohol and marijuana (33% of the sports participants who used marijuana; 27% of those who used beer; 55% of those athletes who drank liquor). When these youth elaborated upon this limitation of use, the major concern was that they not "mess up" their bodies[15] and/or performance *during the sport season*. The following are illustrative excerpts:

> Um, I used to [play sports when high], but I, you know, I really, I'd rather do it straight. Uh, 'cause you're — I'm more competitive, I mean, I like to do, you know, I like to get my mind all clear, when I'm doing stuff, so I can concentrate . . . I think it [pot] affects my performance [makes it] worse. Like after school, we used to sometimes go get high before we go to practice, you know — I don't think you are, I don't think your mind is up to where, you know, up to par about what's happening. [#147]

> Yeah, I cut down a little, I cut down every year, you know, like when it comes to, like track all right, like we have to run, run, run, run, but if we smoke we figure we get dizzy or you know, it'll slow

you down, your air, you know, cuts your winds, you know. I slow down. [#130]

Ya, you know, 'cause I be, you know, stoppin' [pot smoking] for like, for one or two months you know, so like get my wind back, you know, but I started joggin', joggin' more often, you know. . . . Like you know, like when I was playin' basketball and track and stuff, you know, 'cause I didn't drink — only on the weekends, like when I'm at a party or something, you know, I'll have two or three beers. [#135]

Football. That's what I mainly [play]. Next year I think I'll play lacrosse too. I, I like, ya know, my drug counselor says that it's good for me to let out energy, you know; but I've always played football, you know, and I've always been an athletic person, that's why I quit smokin' cigarettes. And when football comes I'll quit pot too and drinking. [#150]

Sport involvement then, according to some of the athletes, does serve to limit substance use, apparently at least during the sports season.[16] The excerpts in this chapter exemplify some of the complications of the sport-drug connection mentioned above; they show how explanations of drug nonuse by youth involved in sports compare with the explanations of those not involved; and present apparent evidence that involvement in sports does serve a kind of "temperance" function for some adolescents.

Summary: Nonuse

This section has presented, in the words of the adolescents themselves, the explanations for nonuse (or occasionally limited use) of various substances (i.e., marijuana, beer, liquor, hard drugs). The majority of these explanations related to some type of fear.

For all substances, the explanations for nonuse and limitation of use given by the youth were subsumed under three major themes: generalized fear, fear of harming the body, and fear of addiction. It was only with hard drugs that general fear of permanent damage to one's body and fear of death were mentioned. Other reasons for nonuse of the various substances included the illegality or "wrongness" of substance use, no opportunity to try various substances, no desire to use various substances, and involvement in sports.

While many of the explanations were given by both participants and nonparticipants in sports, there were some differences between the explanations given for nonuse of substances by participants and nonparticipants in sport. Across all substance types more sports participants than nonparticipants indicated an absence of desire to try a substance. In terms of both liquor and beer consumption, it was primarily sports participants who expressed fear of getting sick. Likewise, more athletes explained nonuse of liquor and drugs in terms of the physical effects on their bodies and more sports participants, especially those involved with organized sports, related nonuse of hard drugs to fear of addiction. From this, it would seem, then, that there is some evidence in support of the social myth that sports and a degree of temperance go hand-in-hand.

A possible explanation for these particular differences in the reasons for nonuse of various substances might be found within the institution of sport itself. Sport is a social institution; as is the case with all social institutions, the individuals in that institution are socialized both *into* and *through* the structures of the particular institution. Thus, sports (especially organized sports) convey to their participants messages, values, and beliefs (and fears), either about substance use or about the care and control of one's own body. The values associated with involvement in organized sports — strong, healthy bodies; self-discipline; respect for self, including one's body; respect for others; positive character development and self-development (Bannister, 1973; Edwards, 1973; Friedenberg, 1973; Sugden and Yiannakis, 1982) — imply some sense of self-control, and the particular motor and social skills involved in organized sports require control over one's world, at least the specified world of sport. Addiction is seen as destroying control, both self-control and control of one's world, and is antithetical to the control needed by athletes, especially those involved in organized sports. Thus, learning, through socialization into and through sport, the values associated with sport, may help explain why some participants in organized sports express the fears they do (e.g., effects on the body physiologically, loss of control, addiction), and yet at the same time they may in fact use other drugs (since there is the perception that use of some types of drugs can be controlled or tempered and may even enhance performance).

NOTES

1. The description of situations that often coincided with the adolescents' descriptions of smoking or drinking because it was "fun" is deliberate. It is not necessarily the case that the situation *per se* was fun, but rather that the smoking or drinking was described as fun, and that the smoking or drinking took place within the context of these situations.

2. It can be speculated that perhaps this was not mentioned for alcohol simply because it is so readily available that mentioning availability simply wasn't worthwhile. (The next section notes that not one individual indicated that she/he had no opportunity to use alcohol.)

3. Availability as a reason for use of hard drugs was not as substance-specific as was the case with some of the other reasons for use of hard drugs, and no major pattern seemed to emerge regarding any one specific drug. The adolescents who tried or used any type of harder drug for which availability was a reason did not elaborate beyond the notion that they did it because it was "around."

4. This is not to say that this is the only reason athletes gave for their use of marijuana, but it is a reason given exclusively by athletes.

5. While only a few athletes spoke of the use of a drug to allow continued play while injured, the acknowledgment of this practice and the statement of willingness to take a drug to play while injured is evidence of an issue with which physical educators, researchers, coaches, athletic trainers, parents, and players need to deal.

6. For example, the following is a typical comment regarding the availability of hashish: "Can't get it [hash] around anymore, it's too expensive" [#003].

7. The distinction is being made that there are both substantiated and unsubstantiated fears. If, as was found in this study, fear of the effects of a substance is expressed by both youth with no experience (unsubstantiated) and those with experience (substantiated), perhaps this may suggest that utilizing the fear element in educational programs and publications geared to prevention of drug use or abuse may possibly have some success (although some health education research has shown that fear messages have not been a deterrent to drug and cigarette usage (Antonow et al., 1976; Mathews, 1975).

8. It is interesting to note that 24 percent of the drinkers of beer and/or liquor also revealed that they did not like the taste of the substance.

9. Related to alcohol consumption, one explanation given for the nonuse of beer and wine was that of disliking the substance because of the "nasty taste." Although this reason was expressed by both participants and nonparticipants in sports who were nonusers of alcohol, all of the subjects who spoke of disliking alcoholic substances because of the taste were younger adolescents (15 or under), perhaps indicating that the taste is acquired.

10. Again, it should be noted that while participants in sports offered the types of explanations just mentioned, these explanations were not directly connected with athletic participation, which suggests that perhaps, at least for some of the subjects in this study, athletic involvement (and its stereotypical expectations) is not perceived to have a deterring effect on substance use, at least on alcohol consumption. However, in the discussion of marijuana use in the previous chapter, the preference of marijuana over alcohol related to sports participation may indicate a direct tie between sports and choice of drug to be used.

11. This may indicate that perhaps sports participants may get a different set of messages, or may hold a different set of beliefs, concerning hard drug use/nonuse than those not involved in sports.

12. This is in contrast to the information and fears the youth talk about in relation to alcohol and marijuana; few, if any, speak of school or the movies as their source of information.

13.   Although the number of regular users of harder drugs is small and the types of drugs used varied, this particular fear is not only a pattern among the users in this sample but is also a concern of drug users in general. Thus, even in the world of illicit drug use, it appears that everyday rules concerning consumer expectations hold. Perhaps more vividly and realistically drug users worry about "bad stuff" killing them.

14.   Perhaps this is an indication of different socialization messages reaching athletes, such as concern and respect for one's body. Or perhaps these are different kinds of individuals, or perhaps they are simply busy with different activities.

15.   The discussions of one of the adolescents, a professional speed skater, is interesting for the light it sheds on "limitations" regarding marijuana use. This individual much prefers to play sports when high, but states: "I don't do any drugs when I'm skating. That's like — that's my serious, you know, I won, money and stuff, you know, it's fun and stuff, I like it. And, you know, I don't mean to be conceited but I'm good. You know. I don't, I don't do any kind of drugs at all when I'm skating. 'Cause that's, you know, you got to — crack down, con, concentrate on your stuff" [#037].

16.   While not a focus of concern for this study, it is interesting to note that over half of the athletes who were cigarette smokers indicated that because of their sports involvement, they either quit entirely or cut down substantially the number of cigarettes smoked during their sports season(s). Baugh (1970) also found that athletics had a deterrent effect on smoking. There was more concern about the harm that would or could be done to the body, and the impairment of sports performance, from cigarette smoking than from use of other substances (data from total study, but not reported herein).

6

Theoretical Perspectives Revisited

This study has utilized an interpretive, *verstehen*-oriented approach, employing extensive in-depth interviews in order to explore the place of sports in society, as can be seen in the accounts of adolescents, some of whom are athletes, some of whom are not; and, more specifically, to explore the ways in which drug (including alcohol) use/nonuse fits into the lives of, and is talked about by, youth who participate in sports activities and those who do not. The presentation of the data has been, as far as possible, in the words of the adolescents themselves. This work is an important contribution to the body of knowledge since most previously completed research in this area has utilized survey instruments, which can only scratch the surface of the complexities involved in drug use, and because little or no previous work has dealt with the way in which adolescents talk about (i.e., explain, justify, account for) drug usage.

The preceding chapters have discussed the various specific questions of empirical and theoretical interest in this study. The evidence presented has suggested that, for some adolescents, sports have a most important place and meaning in their lives, and for others it is something not even mentioned in their discussions; that, on the whole, the explanations of drug use/nonuse given by youth involved and not involved in sports are not markedly different. Other questions raised in the study are:

1. Is the popular conception that sports and "clean living" go hand-in-hand, especially among youth, just a myth?

2. Is involvement in sports chosen by some individuals as a means
   by which she/he either seeks to prevent her/his own drug use or
   tries to rehabilitate her/himself?

3. Is such involvement in sports, rather than a mechanism for
   prevention or rehabilitation, a mechanism for "temperance" —
   that is limitation — of kind and/or amount of drug used?

4. What part does the peer group play in an adolescent's social
   world, specifically in relation to drug use/nonuse; and more
   particularly, is sports involvement merely one more type of peer
   group that facilitates and encourages or makes more difficult and
   discourages the use of drugs?

The findings are complex. Some adolescents who are involved in
sports actively used alcohol and other drugs, some specifically for
purposes related to sports performance; other youth specifically chose
sports involvement and/or athletic peers as a way of preventing or
tempering drug use.

Related to this, the evidence supports the contention that sport is an
institution with its own values, beliefs, and norms; it is an agent of social
control, and the adolescents in this study believe, act upon, and include
the myth in their social worlds that sports and "clean living" go hand-in-
hand. However, at the same time, the evidence also suggests that, in fact,
the notion of sports and "clean living" is a myth and that there exists
multiple sets of norms, values, and beliefs related to drug use inherent in
the institution of sport.

The findings show that some youth who were involved in sports not
only used alcohol and other drugs but also used some drugs specifically
for purposes related to sports performance. At the same time, the data
also offered evidence that yet other adolescents (accepting the social myth
mentioned above) chose sports involvement and/or athletic peers as a way
of preventing or tempering substance use. Thus, the findings from this
study are evidence to both support and refute some of the specific
questions posed herein. The following sections will more fully
summarize the findings of the study.

SUMMARY: GENERAL

Initially, the findings of this study indicated that the social worlds of
the sample of youth were not appreciably different: Females and males
differed in terms of some of the types of activities in which they engaged;

athletes and nonathletes differed primarily by virtue of the sports involvement of those designated as athletes. Regardless of classification concerning sports participation or drug use, the youth were almost all in school;
all but a few claimed membership in some religious denomination (even if
they did not actively practice); nearly all indicated that having and spending time with friends was very important; most envisioned having jobs,
usually well-paying, in their futures. Since there is practically no research
that attends to the similarities and differences among and between drug
users and nonusers in terms of their larger social worlds, regardless of
their use or nonuse of drugs, this is an important contribution to the
larger picture, an attempt to begin to identify factors that might affect
substance use and nonuse, including the changing nature of society
(Bedworth, 1971).

DRUGS: USE/NONUSE

When the issue of drug use was examined, in general there were
similarities as well as differences among the adolescents in their
reasons for use/nonuse of drugs. Given the widespread social and
educational concern with teenage alcohol use and its related problems,
of major importance is the finding that *there was not a single adolescent*
who indicated that she or he had had no opportunity to use alcoholic
substances. Sixty-six percent of all the adolescents were users of beer,
52 percent were users of liquor; 55 percent were users of marijuana;
27 percent were users of one or more various hard drugs. In terms of
sports participation and substance use, it was shown in Chapter 4 (Table
4.3) that as level of sports involvement decreased, use of all substances increased. That is, while 50 percent of the organized sports
participants used beer, 75 percent of the recreational sports participants
and 77 percent of all nonparticipants used beer; 28 percent of sports
participants (42 percent of the organized, 54 percent of the recreational)
used marijuana, but 69 percent of nonparticipants used marijuana.[1]
This parallels the work of Hayes and Tevis (1977), Tec (1972) and
Blum et al. (1970), but runs counter to the findings of Moos et al. (1976)
and Rooney (1984). Similarly, the findings of this study support
the popular beliefs, corroborated by much research, that sports participation is likely to produce appropriately socialized citizens who
conform to "conventional" norms[2] (Snyder and Spreitzer, 1979; Segrave
and Chu, 1978; Snyder, 1972; Ferdinand, 1966) and research which
shows that sports participation is likely to deter "delinquent" behavior
(Purdy and Richard, 1983; Segrave, 1983; Snyder and Spreitzer, 1979;

Buhrman, 1977; Rehberg, 1969; Schafer and Armer, 1968; Matza, 1964a).

Reasons for Use

The reasons articulated for drug use by those individuals who used drugs were varied and included: physical effects (i.e., taste, sleep facilitation, enhancement or energy), mental and emotional effects (i.e., to get in a "good mood," to get "mellow"), specific effects (i.e., getting high or drunk and for "fun"); "environmental" factors (i.e., general availability and availability at parties); and "motivational" reasons (i.e., simply wanting to; as a result of boredom, of nothing else to do). The finding that boredom was given as a reason for drug use coincides with that of many other studies (Adams and Resnik, 1985; Wasson, 1981; Minatoya and Sedlacek, 1979; Butler, 1976; O'Connor, 1976; Guinn, 1975; Messolonghites, 1974; Samuels and Samuels, 1975; Cohen, 1973; Spady, 1971; Clinard and Wade, 1966; Briar and Piliavin, 1965; Bordua, 1960; Schafer, 1969a, 1969b). It appears from some of the reasons given for substance use that some individuals who used drugs were lacking stimulation and alternative activities. Such activities might have provided options so that they would not have felt a need for a chemical "high," for drugs as "something to do," or because they were "bored." In contrast it can be speculated that athletes had "more to do" — that is, were less bored and thus were less involved in substance use.

Athletes mentioned one unique reason for use of marijuana: Some believed that being high while engaged in sports enhanced performance. Likewise only athletes mentioned the use of codeine, and predominantly athletes mentioned the use of speed for specific purposes in relation to sport. This parallels the findings of Baugh (1970) related to substance use, and the findings of Leonard (1984) concerning the use of drugs for "additive" — that is, enhancement — and "restorative" — that is, the alleviation of pain or injury — purposes.

Reasons for Nonuse

Adolescents who did not use marijuana gave several types of reasons for their nonuse: generalized, nonspecific fear (e.g., being "scared"); fear of harming one's body (e.g., cancer); fear of addiction. For nonusers of beer and nonusers of liquor, the explanations included: fear of loss of control; fear of effects on the body (e.g., "sloppy, falling down"; "eats up your insides"; getting sick). Nonusers of hard drugs offered the following explanations: generalized fear (e.g., "freakin' out", "gettin' messed up"); fear of harming one's body (e.g., "harming your organs," death); fear of addiction.

Most of these adolescents (i.e., those who expressed the above-mentioned fears), when specifically asked where they obtained their information, indicated that they learned about drugs and alcohol and their effects and, thus their fears, from the movies and/or from health classes. The data indicate that indeed the lessons, films, discussions, and the like from health classes were one source of information that influenced some adolescents to temper their use of drugs. In fact, the "fear" tactics of presentation, criticized a number of years ago (Antonow et al., 1976; Mathews, 1975) seemed to work, given these youths' accounts, for some in this study. Many expressed fears of becoming "junkies" or addicts and fear of using needles, based upon films seen in health classes.[3]

THE PEER GROUP

The findings of this study show that in almost all cases there was a similarity between the adolescent's peer group's use or nonuse and the adolescent's own use/nonuse of a given substance; this supports a number of previously cited works related to this topic (Mensch and Kandel, 1988; Pisano and Rooney, 1988; Silverman, 1987; Adams and Resnik, 1985; American Association of School Administrators, 1985; Hawkins et al., 1985; Blount and Dembo, 1984; Kaplan et al., 1984; Rooney, 1984; Rugg and Jaynes, 1983; Sarvela and McClendon, 1983; Rooney, 1982-83; Biddle et al., 1980b; Kandel, 1980; Akers et al., 1979; Levine and Kozak, 1979; Ginsberg and Greenley, 1978; Kandel et al., 1978; Jessor and Jessor, 1977; Lucas et al., 1975; Forslund and Gustafson, 1970). For example, if an individual was a regular user of beer, most of her/his peer group were also regular users; if an individual was a nonuser, most of her/his peer group were also nonusers. Similarly, the findings also reveal that several youth deliberately changed peer groups to increase substance use, and a few others consciously changed peer groups (most often to an athletically oriented group) in order to cut down, eliminate, or prevent their own involvement with drugs. This corroborates the work of Johnson et al. (1986), Brown (1982), Conger (1980), and Biddle (1980a).

SPORTS PARTICIPATION

Sports participation was an important part of the lives of many of the youth in this study: 70 percent of the males and 42 percent of the females were classified as athletes. For these youth, sport was an activity in which they spent time generally (free time as well as practices and games), leaving little free time in which to get bored; and sport was a vehicle for spending time with friends. Likewise, for 33 percent of the male sports participants (and only one female), sport was a life goal of some sort.

On another level, in terms of substance use, the athletic peer group was one specific peer group to which some adolescents changed when they wished an alternative to substance use. Still other adolescents (20 percent of male sports participants) indicated that it was specifically *their own* personal involvement in sports programs that helped them avoid drugs. This lends support to the notion that athletes tend to be less "delinquent," corroborating the findings of Research & Forecasts (1983); Segrave (1983); Segrave and Hastad (1982); Segrave (1981a, 1981b); Buhrman and Bratton (1978); Buhrman (1977); Landers and Landers (1977); Fagerberg and Fagerberg (1976); Schafer (1969a, 1969b). However, it runs counter to the findings of Yiannakis (1981), McCann et al. (1977), Sutherland and Cressey (1955), and Tappen (1949), which states that sports participation plays no role in deterring delinquent behavior; and to the work of Santomier et al. (1980), Segrave and Chu (1978), and Lueschen (1976), which concluded that sports involvement may in fact promote various forms of "deviant" behavior.[4]

For some of the youth so involved, sports (either organized sports or activities in gym class) were an important factor as far as school was concerned: Physical education was often mentioned as the favorite subject of many of the youth; participation on a sports team was given as a reason to stay in school or to refrain from being truant. This finding relates to earlier work citing sports as a vital and integral part of the school curriculum (Alvarado in Rhoden, 1984; McIntosh, 1971; Coleman, 1965; Waller, 1965; Educational Policies Commission, 1964; Fichter, 1961; AAHPER, 1954).

Obviously, the foregoing summary of the findings of this study indicates the evidence needed to answer some of the specific questions raised by this study unequivocally yes or no is not forthcoming, because matters appear more complex. Likewise, the evidence pertaining to the broader theoretical issues of the study is also complex. To tie these findings to broader theoretical perspectives, several theories mentioned in Chapter 2 will be re-addressed in this chapter. The goodness of fit between the data and some of these theories will be presented; these theories will be used to explain certain findings, and findings will be used to comment upon theoretical concepts.

LEARNING THEORIES

Relevant findings from the study will be discussed in this section, in light of two traditional learning theories: Sutherland's theory of differential association (1939) and Cohen's subcultural theory (1955).[5] Given the global nature of these theories, specific claims will not necessarily be discussed; however, findings supporting the general theoretical contribution of each will be discussed.

Differential Association

Sutherland's theory of differential association (1939), which incorporates learning theory as well as behavioral dimensions, has helped to inform all of the specific research questions of this study. To reiterate, the essence of differential association is that an individual is more likely to become similar to certain types of individuals the more the individual associates with them. Since differential association can help to explain both routine, conventional behavior as well as routine, "delinquent" behavior, such as drug use,[6] this theory may be examined for the general conceptual fit with the data. Each of the major areas of this study demonstrated particular types of differential association and thus provided support for this generalized learning theory.

First and quite broadly, the youth in this study appear to have "learned" what it means to be an adolescent (rather than an adult) in the late twentieth century in the United States. The findings presented in Chapter 4 provided evidence for this general type of social learning. While it was shown that the social worlds of the adolescents in this study were not appreciably different in that, in general, athletes and nonathletes were indistinguishable in terms of their social worlds, there was a major and noticeable distinction — that being sports involvement by those youth who did so participate. Related to this was the associated finding that as athletic participation increased, substance use decreased. From this latter finding, it can be inferred that as association with sports participants increased, some type of differential learning relevant to drug use and/or sports may have occurred, specifically within the context of the athletic association or associates. Perhaps, as a result of this differential association with athletes and the presumed differential learning, drug use itself then may be decreased.

In a larger sense, the adolescents in this study, regardless of how they can be categorized on the basis of sports participation or drug use, also have "learned" the social values of the larger world. For example, all but a few of them were still in school[7]; most of them spoke of having jobs (and they hoped well-paying jobs) when asked about life goals and what a good day ten years in the future would look like; all but a few of them claimed membership in some religious denomination (even though they might not actively practice the religion). Similarly, it was shown in Chapter 4 that the adolescents in this study have also "learned" the myth of the larger social world concerning the marriage of sports and "clean living." The adolescents in this study, regardless of their actual behavior, did make distinctions between "druggies" and "jocks," between those who used various drug substances and those involved in sports who were assumed or expected not to use alcohol and other drugs. The use of such language is further evidence of learning the values and beliefs both from the larger social world and from within their own adolescent world, for such terms are used both popularly and within the adolescent subculture. The adolescents used and had common meanings for terms such as "druggies," "burnouts," "jocks." These shared meanings and a "common special language" are evidence of both the learning of the social values of the larger world as well as that of a shared subculture, specifically the adolescent subculture within which these various types of persons are found (cf. Eckert, 1989, Selakovich, 1984).

Looking at differential association more specifically in relation to the categories of sports participant/nonparticipant and drug use, there was evidence to support the concept of different learnings because of membership in two differentially associated categories. There were some different explanations for some types of drug use given by members of the two different groups (i.e., athletes and nonathletes). For instance, while athletes and nonathletes who used alcohol and other drugs had essentially quite similar explanations for their use/nonuse of alcohol and marijuana, a marked difference in explanations was evident in terms of hard drug use. Athletes who used hard drugs (e.g., codeine, speed) had sport-specific reasons for their use of these drugs (e.g., to kill pain, to enhance performance, to stay awake); nonathletes had no such specific reasons. Origins of the reasons and explanations for use were not articulated nor systematically requested by the interviewer; however, it may be speculated that the different explanations were due to differential learning because of the sports participants' association with athletes and athletics (and the types of learning that occur through sports socialization), and the nonparticipants' lack of such association. That is, each of these types of adolescents engaged in behaviors and activities they defined as appropriate to their situation (sports participant or nonparticipant). Since only participants in sports gave these sport-specific reasons for the use of hard drugs, it can be speculated that perhaps they did, in fact, learn about these uses because of association with athletes and athletics. Also related to this issue, it is speculated that the athletes "learned" something from the larger social and athletic world about sport-specific drug use, given the media coverage of drug scandals and crises within the sports world around the time the interviews were conducted.[8]

The findings related to the gender differences in the activities of the adolescents and findings related to the peer group are more in suppport of differential association by sex and peer group than any based upon categorization by sports participant/nonparticipant. Specifically, in terms of the activities of the adolescents, it was shown (Chapter 4) that girls appeared to be more sedentary than boys, preferring such activities as watching TV or movies, reading or writing, singing, or playing musical instruments and shopping, none of which were mentioned by many boys; similarly, girls (even sports participants) did not *mention* playing sports as a way in which they spent their free time or time with friends. Boys in contrast mentioned drinking, smoking marijuana, and getting rowdy, which were mentioned by very few girls. Again, it appears that each of these types of adolescents engaged in behavioral acts they defined as appropriate to their situation — i.e., gender role. Thus it would appear that some differential learning occurred for the sexes, given these differences in activities. This is not meant to imply that girls necessarily *behaviorally* differentially associated (i.e., engaged in these activities with other girls) for obviously several of these activities are solitary activities (e.g., reading or writing) but rather that differential learning occurred, learning which suggested that these are the types of activities which girls (more so than boys) do (or *say* they do), and/or talk about (e.g., shopping). In contrast, the activities that boys mention, but girls do not, suggest that both behavioral differential association (i.e., activities engaged in with other boys) and differential learning may have occurred, because the boys' activities (e.g., drinking, getting rowdy) are the types of activities boys (more so than girls) engage in (or *say* they do), and/or talk about. These findings support both the behavioral component and the learning component of differential association.

The findings pertaining to the peer group, specifically the peer group and drug use/nonuse, also support the theoretical concepts of differential association. As was mentioned in Chapter 4, users of various drugs reported that their friends also used the substance under discussion; quite frequently, they also indicated that it was the peer group that served as the impetus to the individual's starting to use the substance; it is also this group within which the individuals learned how to smoke, drink, and so on. This finding is supportive of differential association generally, and in fact supports as least two of Sutherland's nine propositions, namely: "(1) criminal [delinquent] behavior is learned; (2) criminal [delinquent] behavior is learned in interaction with persons in a process of communication" (Sutherland and Cressey, 1955:77).

Likewise, individuals who had only experimented with drugs generally had peers who had only experimented with the substance under question. Individuals who were nonusers had peers who were nonusers, and these individuals were usually emphatic in their statements about their own unwillingness to "hang around" with people who did use drugs, and very frequently contained references to sports and athletes' nonuse of drugs. This again seems to offer evidence supporting differential association, both the behavioral and the learning component.

A number of the youth reported consciously chosen changes in their peer groups, some to a peer group that was more actively involved in substance use. The choice to change one's peer group implied the willingness and/or desire to learn about and/or share in "delinquent" behaviors and explanations for these behaviors. This then seems to offer additional support to differential association theory's claim that individuals engage in behaviors (acts) that they define as appropriate to their situation (drug user/nonuser). Conversely, other individuals also made a choice to change peer groups, but these adolescents either chose to change peer groups in order to curtail their own substance use or reported a curtailment of use because of the group to which they had changed. Either case offers evidence in support of differential association.

In sum, then, the findings from this study tend to support some of the propositions made by Sutherland, as well as the more general behavioral and learning components of learning theory.

Subcultural Theory

Related to the general notion of learning theory, and specifically to Sutherland's idea of differential association, is Cohen's concept of subculture (1955). As noted in Chapter 2, Cohen argued that delinquents form their own subculture based upon possession of a value system directly in opposition to the dominant culture; he described that subculture as one that takes "its norms from the larger culture but turns them upside down. The delinquent's conduct is right, by the standards of his subculture precisely because it is wrong by the norms of the larger cultures" (Cohen, 1955:28).[9]

Further, the general conception of subculture includes the following points:

1. A subculture is characterized by the interaction of its members especially so that

2. Interaction with others not in possession of these shared interests is reduced;

3. Social interaction within the subcultural group(s) results in the individuals manifesting behaviors, attitudes, beliefs, etc. characteristic of the subculture (Donnelly, 1981b; Pearson, 1981; Shibutani, 1955).

Thus the concept of subculture appears to be particularly useful to explain the findings, and appears to be supported by them.

The findings of this study presented somewhat mixed evidence concerning distinctive subcultural differences among various groups. First, since both sports participants and nonparticipants used drugs, there did not appear to be any subcultural delineation between athletes, presumably a "nondeviant" group, and nonathletes based upon substance use: Both shared the common interest in drug use (however, to different degrees). It does appear, however, that there is in fact a subculture based upon sports participation: Those who participated in sports shared that common interest and formed one subculture; those who did not participate in sports formed another kind of subculture, namely one based upon *not* participating in sports. However, as mentioned above, members of both the sports subculture and the nonsport subculture were members of still another subculture, either a drug-using subculture or a nonuse subculture. In addition, all would be considered members of the adolescent subculture.

Utilizing the second characteristic of subcultures — interaction of its members, especially so that interaction with others not in possession of these shared interests is reduced — it appears that sports participants and nonparticipants were distinctive subcultures, using sports involvement as the critical interest factor. However, individuals might belong to several subcultures based upon the sharing of other interests and interaction in other mutually named activities (e.g., drug use/ nonuse, activities which occupy free time — "hanging out," listening to music, etc.). These other shared interests, rather than negating the notion of sports participant/nonparticipant subcultures, attest to the *multiplicity* of subcultures to which an individual might belong (e.g., adolescent, athlete, drug user, athletic nondrug user, etc.). Figure 6.1 presents schematically some of the possible subcultural variations.

Figure 6.1
Some Possible Subcultural Variations

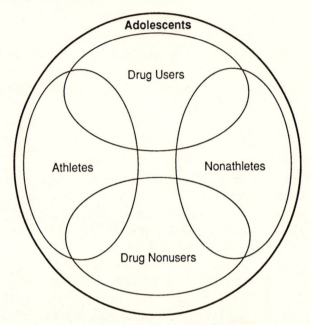

On yet another level, sports involvement was the mechanism by which individuals made friends, often "special" friends, and was a mechanism for some that facilitated "temperance" or avoidance of drug use. Sports participants, by virtue of the essence and meaning of sport, then, were in some senses members of a particular subculture, for they shared (and were perceived by others to share) and accepted a set of conventional rules and values. Similarly, the distinctions that both athletes and nonathletes made between people they called "druggies" and people they called "jocks" are evidence of implied subcultural distinctions between athletes and nonusers of drugs.

Nonetheless, individuals who used drugs, whether involved in sports or not, gave many of the same types of explanations for their drug use, reflective of similar attitudes and beliefs regarding drug use. Here there were no apparent exclusive subcultural learnings, values, attitudes, beliefs, and so on, related to drug use that distinguished athletes and nonathletes. This similarity of explanation and behavior provided evidence, based upon this third characteristic of subcultures, for the existence of a drug-using subculture that shared similar explanations and accounts, cutting across the boundaries of athletic and nonathletic subcultures.

However, where there were different types of explanations for use or nonuse of substances (specifically, marijuana, speed, and codeine), these different explanations were offered by athletes. In this case, it can be postulated that learning appears to have taken place within that distinct sports subculture the content of which is that certain drugs are (or are perceived to be) helpful in the performance of one's sport. These and the findings mentioned earlier (e.g., the distinction between "druggies" and "jocks") seem to support both McPherson's (1981) and Kenyon and McPherson's (1981) position that sport is an agent of socialization, through which values, expectations, norms, and modes of behavior may be learned, and Phillips and Schafer's (1971) concept that a distinct subculture of athletes exists because two of the essential elements of a subculture — special experiences and high rates of interaction — exist among athletes. As will be seen below, the essence of sports participation, especially team sports, requires interaction and involvement and provides special experiences related to that interaction and involvement, attachment and commitment, thus fulfilling the criteria for a subculture mentioned earlier.

Nonetheless, related to the above-mentioned criticisms of the concept of subculture and the complexities noted in the foregoing sections, of import to this study is the fact that the social worlds of both athletes and nonathletes were, except for the participation in sports by those youth who did so participate, and the involvement in drugs by those youth so involved, basically indistinguishable. Thus, from one perspective, the youth in this study appear not to be subculturally different (e.g., all are part of an adolescent subculture); from other perspectives there do appear to be further subcultural breakdowns by athletic participation, drug use, or sex. These differences reflect reality and these may be important differences, subcultural differences, in a *variety* of aspects of the lives of these adolescents.

However, with the exceptions noted, there are no major differences between participants and nonparticipants in sports, nor are there many distinct differences among the youth as a whole (except perhaps gender differences in terms of the activities they report as occupying their free time). Thus, in regard to the youths' social worlds in total, if adolescence can be defined as a subculture, based upon the characteristics listed above, the findings do lend support to the *general* notion of subculture. Further, the findings are indicative of the fact that there is a *multiplicity* of subcultures to which adolescents can and do belong (see Figure 6.1). From this perspective, then, there is a convincing goodness of fit between the data and the theoretical concept of subculture as an agent of learning shared values, behaviors, and explanations.[10]

Social Control Theories

The learning theories, both Sutherland's differential association theory and Cohen's subcultural theory, actually are forerunners of the more specific social control theories that have been developed to help explain delinquency and crime, since the latter imply the learning of social or cultural values and expectations. For example, if one is "bonded" to society (Hirschi, 1969), one certainly has learned and accepted the values of the society. Likewise, if one must use neutralization techniques because one cannot be "totally immune from the demands for conformity made by the dominant social order" (Sykes and Matza, 1957:665), then it follows that one has already learned what those demands are. Thus, this section will deal with two of these more particular social control theories, namely Hirschi's control theory (1969) and Matza's (1964a) and Sykes and Matza's (1957) neutralization theory. This section will discuss the fit between the data and each of these theories; more specifically, this section will present evidence to tie Hirschi's theoretical perspective to the data, and will present evidence relating Matza's neutralization theory to the findings of the study.

Control Theory. In his control theory, Hirschi maintains that "delinquent" behavior (e.g., drug use) is linked to the bond that an individual maintains with society. If that bond weakens or is broken, society's constraints are lifted and the individual may violate the law, and youth may engage in delinquent acts.[11] According to Hirschi there are four main elements of the social bond: (1) attachment (sensitivity to and interest in others), with attachment to parents, peers, and schools being most important; (2) commitment (time, energy, and effort expended in conventional behaviors); (3) involvement (time spent as a result of commitment), which serves as a foil to delinquent behavior; and (4) belief (acceptance of conventional rules and values).[12]

For Hirschi, the *critical* form of attachment was defined as attachment to parents and family; however, this is a very limited definition of "attachment" for it fails to recognize the importance of school and peers (although Hirschi does admit that these are among the most important socializing institutions). These two areas — school and peers — are two facets of social life with which adolescents are most familiar and with which they spend a great deal of time, with which there is a great deal of interaction and "attachment." Thus, as was mentioned in Chapter 2, for this study "attachment" was defined as involvement in sports activities that encompass attachment to peers and/or school, thus expanding the notion of attachment into areas and persons of import to adolescents (i.e., school and peers). In general, the findings of this study provided evidence of the concepts that constitute the individual elements of the social bond as Hirschi and others have defined and interpreted them. However, the theory as a whole received inconclusive support from the data and goodness of fit was lacking, since even youth who were "bonded" to the dominant society (i.e., were attached, committed, involved, and apparently believed in the values of the larger society) engaged in the societally defined "delinquent" behaviors of adolescent alcohol and drug use.

As was mentioned, evidence for each of the elements of the social bond was noted in the data, especially for athletes. Since the elements of attachment and belief are closely related, they are presented together. The elements of attachment and belief were examined primarily within the context of involvement in sports. The findings revealed that for many of the youth, sports involvement was a mechanism by which they made friends, often "special" friends. Sports participants are in many ways very "conventional" individuals, for they share and accept a set of conventional rules and values. Participation in sports, especially organized sports, is also evidence of attachment to conventional groups and institutions. As was mentioned in Chapter 4, for some individuals, it was sports and sports alone for which respondents stayed in school, and physical education was, for others, their favorite subject.

However, it was not only in relation to involvement in sports that the elements of the social bond about which Hirschi speaks were demonstrated. As mentioned elsewhere, the youth in this study, regardless of participation/nonparticipation in sports or use/nonuse of alcohol and other drugs, all indicated various forms of involvement with their friends as an important element of their social worlds. This, as well as involvement in sports, is evidence of attachment and belief, again owing to the sharing of similar values (perhaps different among and between the groups, but similar within groups and within the adolescent world as a whole). Thus, the findings of this study provide evidence of the elements of control theory that Hirschi called attachment and belief.

Involvement and commitment are likewise closely related elements of the social bond, and in some senses constitute the behavioral component of attachment. Participation in sports is very much a "conventional" activity — that is, a socially accepted, approved, and expected activity, which encompasses the teaching and learning of "correct attitudes and the

transmission of basically conservative, status quo values of society"
(Schafer, 1971). Sports participation is also often a conventional goal of
young people, especially males, involvement in which requires
expenditure of time, energy, and effort and requires a high degree of
commitment. Thus, involvement in sports specifically demonstrates these
elements of the social bond. The findings of the study show further that
even youth who were not committed and involved in conventional
activities through sports involvement were committed to and involved to
some degree with conventional goals, as was seen for example in their
comments about the future: most of them were still in school and when
asked, most of them claimed to belong to a religious sect or
denomination. As was the case with attachment and belief, the findings of
this study demonstrated the elements of commitment and involvement
included in Hirschi's control theory.

Related to the individual elements of control theory, which have just
been discussed, there are several specific claims that Hirschi makes
concerning his theory. These specific claims (Hirschi, 1969:23, 159,
190) are as follows:

(a) [T]he leisure of the adolescent produces a set of values,
which, in turn, leads to delinquency.

(b) There is a very strong tendency for boys to have friends
whose activities are congruent with their own attitudes.

(c) Most "conventional" activities . . . neither inhibit nor
promote [delinquency].[13]

The evidence from this study does not appear to support claim (a)
above. The values of the adolescents, as inferred from their discussions
and explanations of their various activities, appear to be "typical"
American values. The youth valued (at least appeared to value) education,
as seen in the fact that most were still in school and many planned to
continue on to college; they valued spirituality, in that most claimed
membership in some religion and believed in God; they valued success,
especially as measured by money, since they all had goals of having well-
paying jobs at some time in the future; they valued friends and
friendships, as seen in the number of adolescents who indicated that
spending time with or talking with friends was a way they spent their
time. Some of the youth quite emphatically spoke of the way in which
they valued their bodies and/or minds and how they participated in sports
and/or did not use drugs in order to protect body and mind. Most of these
values were shared by nearly all of the adolescents, even those who

engaged in the "delinquent" activity of drug use. On the other hand, for a few of those who did use drugs, boredom was a reason given for substance use. Boredom may, in fact, be a result of the leisure available to adolescents; however, given that most of these adolescents seemed to be involved in other activities (e.g., music, reading, shopping, etc.) reflective of conventional values, it is difficult to conclude that leisure which may produce boredom leads to values which lead to "delinquency." Thus, while the very (stereotypical) nature of adolescence may produce leisure not usually available to some other age groups, in this study there is little evidence to support Hirschi's claim that the "leisure of the adolescent produces a set of values, which, in turn, leads to delinquency."

On the other hand, Hirschi's claim (b), "boys [and girls] [tend] to have friends whose activities are congruent with their own attitudes," appears to be supported by the data. For example, as seen in earlier chapters, youth who used drugs had friends who used drugs; youth who did not had friends who did not use drugs; athletes tended to have athletes for friends. At the same time, however, as seen earlier in this chapter, there are probably a multiplicity of subcultures (i.e., groups of friends) to which the youth belong, thus a multiplicity of attitude sets that the youth hold and cross-cutting friendship groups to which they belong. Thus, based on the findings of this study, claim (b) appears to be supported.

The evidence seems to strongly support Hirschi's final claim that "most conventional activities . . . neither inhibit nor promote [delinquency]." The majority of the youth in this study are involved in a number of conventional activities — for example, school, religion, sports, and so on. The involvement in these activities and the apparent concomitant acceptance of "conventional" norms and values seem to have no effect one way or another on the "delinquent" activity of drug use: Some athletes used drugs, some nonathletes did not use drugs; individuals who claimed membership in a religion as well as those who did not used and did not use drugs, and so on. This finding conflicts with conclusions of other researchers and policymakers who propose (or evaluate) programs of so-called conventional activities to deter delinquents.

In summary, given the similarities in most of the activities of the social worlds of the adolescents in this study, the findings presented evidence that supported the existence of each of the *individual elements* of the social bond proposed by Hirschi in his social control theory, and that supported two of the three specific claims mentioned above. However, the essential argument of Hirschi's control theory is that as the social bond weakens (i.e., these elements weaken), delinquency may occur.[14]

As was seen in Table 4.3, as participation in sports declines, regularity of use of all substances increases. Thus, as the attachment element of the social bond (measured here by sports participation) lessens, "delinquent" activity in the form of drug use appears to increase.[15]

The data from this study show that even adolescents who are "bonded" to the society through their attachment, belief, involvement, and commitment in sports activities (see reference to Schafer, 1971, above); through their attachment to friends and peers and their commitment, belief, attachment, and involvement with conventional activities (e.g., school, jobs, religion, job and family-related goals), engage to some degree in the "delinquent" behaviors of alcohol and other drug use. Involvement in such "conventional" activities can neither be shown unequivocally to inhibit nor to promote delinquency.[16, 17] However, since this study was qualitative and captured adolescents at a given point in time, it was difficult, given the study's design, to determine total fit with Hirschi's complete theory, rather than simply its specific elements. Most respondents, even those who used drugs, would be classified as "bonded to conventional society," therefore it would be difficult to determine what they would do if the existent bonds were weakened. Also, since this study only looked at drug taking and drug-taking behaviors and explanations (certainly only one type or category of "delinquent" activity), further work might explore whether other delinquent behaviors were engaged in by those "less bonded" to conventional society.[18]

Thus, the findings as they relate generally to Hirschi's control theory, appear to be inconclusive. The data: (1) support the theory in that as the attachment bond (defined here as participation in sports) is lessened, involvement in drug use increases, and (2) apparently do *not* support the theory in that even those individuals who are bonded to society via other routine and "conventional" activities (in addition to, as well as through, sports) also are involved to some degree with the "delinquent" activity of drug use. It is the opinion of the author that social control theory as advocated by Hirschi is beset with problems. These problems are related to: (1) lack of conceptual clarity of terms such as "weakening of social bonds" and "conventional society"; (2) a major conceptual and theoretical weakness in the use of parental attachment as a measure of attachment, given widely accepted adolescent developmental tasks; and (3) the fact that the same data can be used and interpreted to support or not to support the theory, suggesting that the theory needs further clarification to make it more useful (by the traditional measures of scientific canon — of course, this can probably be said of most theories).

Neutralization Theory. Neutralization theory posits that individuals spend their lives on a continuum somewhere between complete freedom and complete restraint in the American society, a complex pluralistic culture, and that in order to be able to commit "criminal" or "delinquent" acts, legal expectations must be "negated" or neutralized. Neutralization theory then, in contrast with Hirschi's control theory which sees the youthful "delinquent" as someone who has rejected social norms, holds the view that "nondelinquents" and "delinquents" share the same basic values and attitudes, since the latter cannot be "totally immune from the demands for conformity made by the dominant social order" (Sykes and Matza, 1957:665).

The same evidence that supports the individual elements of, and provides inconclusive support for, the social control theory which Hirschi has developed also supports the essence of neutralization theory as developed by Matza. The adolescents in this study did conform to the expectations of those involved in sports; all have various groups of friends; several have jobs; many claim membership in a religious denomination, even though they may not be active members; most have future goals of good-paying jobs, possessions, and spouses, and the like. At the same time, many of these youth also consume alcohol and use other drugs, activities which have traditionally been thought of as "delinquent" by the dominant culture.[19]

Turning to the more specific "techniques" of neutralization which Matza and Sykes have identified, two in particular were most useful in dealing theoretically with the findings of this study, and specifically with the finding that adolescents who were participants in sports (a nondeviant, conventional activity, an activity which is part of the expectations of the larger social order) used alcohol and other drugs.

The technique of denial of injury can be applied to the explanations the adolescents gave for their use of alcohol and other drugs. Adolescents in this study who used alcohol and other drugs often spoke of the knowledge they had of the substances, knowledge frequently obtained from health education classes in school. Part of this knowledge about alcohol and other drugs dealt with their effects on the body and/or mind, effects which the youth were able to talk about and appeared to *intellectually* accept. However, many of these same individuals who knew of the negative effects of the various substances *at the same time used those very substances.* As Sykes and Matza state (1957:667-68), there is no suggestion that this technique of denial of injury "involves an explicit dialectic," rather the adolescent appears to "feel that [her] his behavior does not really cause any great harm despite the fact that it runs counter" to her/his knowledge of the substance. And, in fact, as was shown, many of the adolescents had very explicit, "positive" reasons for their use of substances (e.g., for fun, mood enhancement, etc.), even when they possessed information about potential negative effects.

Similarly, evidence of use of the technique of denial of injury can also be found in the explanations athletes gave for the use of marijuana and for the use of codeine and speed. Athletes, just like other adolescents, received information concerning effects of alcohol and various other drugs from their health education classes and the media. Athletes also may have received other types of information and/or rules and expectations during their socialization into and through sports participation — for example, information concerning training and development of one's body and information concerning the harmful effects of alcohol and other drugs on the body as this particularly affects athletic performance. That some athletes specifically smoked marijuana to enhance sports performance and some athletes used codeine and speed specifically to alleviate pain and enhance performance, respectively, supports this notion of the technique of the denial of injury, specifically injury to themselves, their bodies, and their sports performance.[20]

The technique of appeal to higher loyalties related to most of the explanations adolescents gave regarding their substance use, regardless of participation in sports. As Sykes and Matza (1957:669) state:

> Social controls may be neutralized by sacrificing the demands of the larger society for the demands of the smaller social groups to which the delinquent belongs such as the sibling pair, the gang, or the friendship clique. . . . The most important point is that deviation from certain norms may occur not because the norms are rejected but because other norms, held to be more pressing or involving a higher loyalty, are accorded precedence.

Thus, while the adolescents conformed to many of the norms held by the larger society, while they were knowledgeable about the harmful effects of alcohol and various other drugs, while if athletes they may have conformed to norms of other adolescent groups like the athletic team, in the final analysis, for those youth who drank or used drugs, the group whose norms appeared to be most important was that in which the adolescent drank or used other drugs. This group and its norms were the locus of the "higher authority" to which the adolescents who drank or used other drugs conformed. The explanations offered earlier (e.g., "everybody else is doing it," use at parties, similar usage patterns of the individual and her/his peers) provide evidence to this effect.[21]

Several other types of explanations or techniques of neutralization, based upon the work of Sykes and Matza (1957) and the work of Scott and Lyman (1968), have been further developed by Weinstein (1980). These, like Matza's original list of techniques, fit well within the data, and the data in turn lend support to the typology. Three of Weinstein's types of accounts are most useful: appeal to defeasibility, appeal to psychological drives, and appeal to social pressures.

Support for the technique of appeal to defeasibility is seen in the various explanations offered for drug use categorized as "environmental" factors — that is, the general availability of all substances and the specific availability of drugs at parties. (In terms of availability of alcohol, as was mentioned previously, every adolescent in the study indicated that she/he had had opportunities to consume alcohol.) Explanations classified as this particular technique of neutralization account for and/or blame drug use on general conditions and social situations that make drug use probable (Weinstein, 1980:580). That is, the fact that various drugs (especially alcohol and marijuana) are readily available and that the adolescents indicate plenty of opportunity to use these constitute the "general conditions" which make drug use probable; the parties to which the youth refer are a kind of specific "social situation" that makes drug use almost a "given."

Another technique is that of appeal to psychological drives: Weinstein states that this is an "especially popular account because . . . 'everyone knows' psychoactive substances have the capacity to affect nervousness," anxiety, moodiness, insecurity, and so on (Weinstein, 1980:581). Many of the adolescents in this study offered explanations of drug use categorized as "mental and emotional effects" that included use of drugs to get in a "good mood," to "relax," to get "mellow."

The last of Weinstein's techniques of neutralization to be cited here is the appeal to social pressure. This type of explanation, like appeal to defeasibility, is also related to social conditions and "attributes drug use to social or environmental stresses" (Weinstein, 1980:581). The data fit this explanation and vice versa, in that those reasons categorized as "motivational" are of this nature — namely, some individuals who used drugs and stated they did so simply because it was "something to do," something their peers were doing, or because they were bored. (Chapter 5 presented extensive discussion including examples of these types of explanations.)

While all of these various explanations were offered by all types of adolescent, it should be noted that for some of the athletes, the use of the techniques of neutralization appeared to be somewhat complex. For many of the athletes, these techniques were, in effect, employed only during the nonsport season, for they did not drink or use drugs during the season; for others, the techniques were applied at selective times (e.g., they only drank or got high on the weekends if it was during their sport season). For other athletes, the techniques applied only to specific drugs (e.g., marijuana, speed, codeine for use for specific purposes related to sports). This is evidence of both denial of injury and appeal to higher loyalties, and also to multiple and *situationally different* loyalties.[22, 23]

In addition to the fit of various techniques of neutralization with the data, several specific claims from the work of Sykes and Matza (1957), Mitchell and Dodder (1983), and Weinstein (1980) were also explored for their relationship to the findings and vice versa.

The first claim is "that much delinquency is based on what is essentially an unrecognized extension of defenses to crimes, in the form of justifications for deviance that are seen as valid by the delinquent but not by the legal system or society at large" (Sykes and Matza, 1957:666). The data show that the reasons offered for the use of various drugs are without doubt explanations and justifications that are in no respect accepted as valid by the legal system or by the larger social order (e.g., drinking to "get drunk," smoking marijuana to get "high," doing either out of "boredom," etc.). First, the purchase and consumption of alcohol by persons under the age of 19 (in this state, at the time of data collection) was by definition illegal. Thus, strictly speaking, no justification for use would be accepted as valid by the legal system. Secondly, the use of drugs by anyone is illegal, so again any justification for use would be seen as invalid by the legal system.

Some of the other justifications for drug use given by the adolescents included using marijuana and/or alcohol to get in a "good mood," to get "mellow," or to "relax"; simply for "fun," because the individual was at a "party," or because it was "available." In the commonly accepted sense of "the society at large" there seems to exist an "ideal" American norm for adolescent drug use (i.e., it shouldn't occur), and from this perspective, none of the explanations offered by adolescents for their drug (including alcohol) use would be seen as valid by the "society at large."[24]

The second claim is "that techniques of neutralization are critical in lessening the effectiveness of social control" (Sykes and Matza, 1957:669). Despite legal, larger societal, and sometimes peer, constraints against the use of drugs, the findings of this study confirm the well-known fact that adolescents do use drugs. Apparently, then, "the effectiveness of [larger, idealized] social control" has been lessened. That most of the adolescents who use drugs gave some type or types of explanations for use of drugs, explanations which fell into the categories of justifications enumerated by Matza and Weinstein, suggests that such justifications assist in the process of negating legal and societal social controls.[25]

Another specific finding concerning neutralization theory is "that the most frequently used techniques are, in order: Denial of victim, condemnation of the condemner, denial of responsibility, denial of injury, and appeal to higher authority" (Mitchell and Dodder, 1983). Very simply, the findings of this study differed from those of Mitchell and Dodder. In this study, the most frequently used of Matza's techniques were appeal to higher loyalties and denial of injury.[26,27]

On the basis of some of the findings from this study (i.e., that some explanations were given more often by girls — use of alcohol to release inhibitions — some explanations offered almost exclusively by sports participants, etc.), this author would also suggest that in future research not only would it be necessary to refer to the type of delinquency and the specific neutralization technique used to explain it, but it would also be necessary to refer to the type of social actor involved in order that a better understanding of "delinquency" and neutralization be obtained.

A fourth claim, put forth by Weinstein, states "that the use of various techniques attests that the 'user accepts responsibility for breaking the law but disclaims any wrongdoing' and that the users 'believe indulgence is an act that is rationally chosen, pleasurable, and not harmful'" (Weinstein, 1980:582). As far as the first part of this claim is concerned, by definition the use of the various techniques is a way of justifying one's actions and therefore is a method of denying wrongdoing by negating legal and social constraints. Thus, apparently by definition, the adolescents who give justifications for their use of drugs are disclaiming wrongdoing. In terms of the second part of this claim, the evidence provides strong support; many of the reasons given for use of various substances attest to the pleasurable effects sought by the user (e.g., to get high or drunk, to get in a "better mood," to "feel good," to "quench thirst," for "fun," etc.).

The final claim, also of Weinstein, states: "that nonusers claim (among other things) that they 'do not need illicit drugs, are happy with their lives, or have no desire to escape reality'" (Weinstein, 1980:591). Like the previous claim, this last one received strong support from the data; these justifications were found in the data in almost the same form as noted in the reference cited. In fact, one of the most frequent reasons for nonuse offered by youth in this study was simply "no desire."

In sum, Matza's neutralization theory was a more useful theoretical approach for explaining the findings of this study than was Hirschi's control theory. The findings presented evidence that supported many of the assumptions and specific claims and contentions of neutralization theory. As seen in the preceding section, four of the specific claims were supported by the data; for one claim, the findings differed. As far as general assertions were concerned, the adolescents in this study did appear to know and conform to the expectations and demands of the larger social order. These factors all support the assertion of neutralization theory that both "delinquents" and "nondelinquents" share the same basic values and attitudes, which are reflective of the conformity demands of the larger social world.[28]

At the same time, many of these youth also consumed alcohol and used other drugs, activities which have traditionally been thought of as "delinquent" by the dominant culture.[29] That the adolescents both conformed to the larger society and effectively negated, at least temporarily, some of its expectations, information, and norms through their drug use is support for this theory of neutralization. The various techniques of neutralization articulated by Sykes and Matza (1957) and Weinstein (1980) help to explain the findings of this study by providing a schema with which to view the disparate findings of the study, to organize the data into conceptually useful and discrete groupings, and to talk about and explain the accounts given by the youth. These various techniques (e.g., appeal to higher loyalties, denial of injury) were the specific methods by which the adolescents were able to negate societal expectations and to justify their engagement in a "delinquent" activity.

By definition, the accounts given by the adolescents, when examined from the conceptual and theoretical perspective of neutralization theory, are justifications for behaviors that, by their nature (i.e., the illegality of them), "must," in some manner, be justified. The theoretical perspective of neutralization theory, and the specific neutralization techniques, are important tools with which to understand the social world, for as Weinstein (1980:591) points out: "The giving-and-taking of accounts in everyday life represents one of the most fundamental characteristics of the social order. People are continually explaining why they did or did not do something."

Thus, there is much goodness of fit between the data and Matza's theory, since neutralization theory helps to explain the "delinquent" activity of drug use by individuals who in so many other aspects of their lives were conforming to the norms of the larger social order.

SOCIOLOGY OF SPORT

It has been repeatedly stated that sport is a social fact, a major American institution that has a pronounced influence on individuals within this society, thus is an agent of socialization (McPherson, 1981; Kenyon and McPherson, 1981) and social control (Segrave and Chu, 1978). In fact, it has been reported that fully 82 percent of Americans agree that increased participation in sports would greatly reduce teenage crime (Research & Forecasts, 1983:54) and that "kids feel better doing sports than just about any other activity" (*Cortland Standard*, 1989:21). Some of the data from this study appear to support the contention that sport is a major social institution (Loy et al., 1981; Lueschen and Sage, 1981; Snyder and Spreitzer, 1974) and agent of social control. For example, the findings show that some of the adolescents deliberately chose sports involvement and athletes as friends as alternatives to drug use; that the adolescents in this study seemed to accept the myth about the marriage of sports and "clean living" (i.e., absence of drug use), as evidenced in their distinction between "druggies" and "jocks," this despite behavioral evidence to the contrary; that participation in sports served as a mechanism of "temperance" for those athletes who did use alcohol or other drugs, but who either stopped or cut down on the amount of use during the sports season. In contrast, the fact that there were adolescent athletes who did use alcohol and other drugs does not negate the contention that sport is a major social institution with its own set of values, agents, norms (part of which have to do with nondrug use) and an agent of social control because of these proscriptive norms.

These observations simply reflect reality, a reality that suggests that there are different sets of norms and values inherent in the institution of sport, and that the social control function, for some youth, is not abstinence but perhaps temperance. Thus, it appears that the data support the more general theoretical contentions of the sociologists of sport mentioned above that the major institutions, including the institution of sport, play an important role in the maintenance of social order — that is, they are agents of social control.

The data related to the place of drug usage within sports in part corroborate the findings of Leonard (1984). These findings focus upon reasons for drug use by athletes in two broad areas: drugs as "restorative . . . to alleviate injury, pain, hypertension, sickness, and dissipation" and as "additive . . . to enhance performance" (Leonard, 1984:128–130). Evidence from this study concerning drug use by adolescent athletes reveals the same pattern as far as hard drug use is concerned. Specifically, it was shown that codeine was used as a "restorative," to relieve pain from an injury so that the athlete could continue to play; speed was used as an "additive" to enhance performance. Similarly, for some athletes, marijuana had a special use; it too was used as an "additive," the perception being that the use of marijuana enabled the individual to play better or at least to think she/he played better.

Finally, a more general theoretical contribution to the sociology of sport, taking all the various and apparently disparate findings into consideration, is the fact that drug-taking among youth involved in sports appears to be "a behavioral style which interrelates with interpersonal and socio-cultural factors (Huba et al., 1979; Segal et al., 1980), rather than being a "deviant" behavior. The findings suggest that drug usage among individuals involved with sports activities is a behavior that may be in accord with the norms of various groups to which the individual belongs — for example, the larger adolescent peer group, a specific larger drug-using peer group, and/or a general drug-using subgroup within the athletic peer group.

Similarly, the findings also suggest that there is yet another "behavioral style which interrelates with interpersonal and socio-cultural factors" (Huba et al., 1979; Segal et al., 1980), and this refers to the gender differences in terms of activities reported as ways one spent one's time. As was mentioned, girls appeared to be more sedentary than boys, preferring such activities as watching TV or movies, reading or writing, singing or playing musical instruments, and shopping. Boys, in contrast, mentioned such things as drinking, getting rowdy, and playing sports as ways of spending time. These findings seem to be a rather vivid example of behavior styles and activities that reflect sociocultural gender role expectations, especially vis-à-vis sports and physical activity (*Cortland Standard*, 1989).[30]

SUMMARY

This chapter has addressed several broad theoretical perspectives — learning theories (Sutherland, 1939; Cohen, 1955) and social control theories (Hirschi, 1969; Matza, 1964a; Sykes and Matza, 1957) — as well as theoretical areas within the sociology of sport, and has discussed the goodness of fit between the data and these theories.

In sum, since Sutherland's concept of differential association is implicit in each of the more specific theories, there was a good fit between this general learning theory and the data. Likewise, the evidence from the study fit well with Cohen's theoretical perspective in *general*, especially if one keeps in mind that there may be a *multiplicity* of subcultures to which adolescents can and do belong. Evidence for Hirschi's social control theory, as a whole, was inconclusive, even though when taken individually, each of the particular elements of the social bond about which Hirschi speaks was evidenced in the data. By far the most useful in explaining the data was Matza's neutralization theory, given that the adolescents exhibited a wide range of behaviors conforming to the dominant cultural expectations and at the same time exhibited "delinquent" behaviors such as smoking marijuana and drinking alcohol, and explained their drug use/nonuse in ways that corresponded to the various techniques of neutralization.[31]

In terms of the theoretical areas within the sociology of sport, the findings attested to the fact that sport is indeed an institution with its own values, beliefs, and norms, and it is an agent of social control. However, the evidence also reflected the existence of *different* sets of norms and values inherent within the institution of sport. The evidence also contributed to the sociology of sport in that it revealed that the adolescents who were involved in sports gave the same types of sport-specific reasons (i.e., "restorative" or "additive" for their drug use as did male professional or Olympic athletes (Leonard, 1984:128–130). As Rooney (1984) suggests, there is no strong negative relationship between sports and drugs. For while sport may stand as the symbolic representation of "good behavior," the fact is that sport is a microcosm of the social world, reflecting the general American profile at any given time (Edwards, 1973), and that at this time in our history, the country is witnessing increased drug usage generally as well as athletically.

Perhaps most important, both theoretically and empirically, the findings reflect the reality, the *multiplicity and complexity*, of the social world of the adolescents in this study.

THEORIES AND RESEARCH: COMMENT AND CRITIQUE

This study has utilized a number of theoretical perspectives, and its findings have been presented in terms of support for, and fit with these various theories. The use of these theories and the presentation of data have provided grounds upon which comment and critique related to several of the theories can be made.

First, a brief comment on learning theory. The findings suggest that a variety of learning (most of which was not "criminal" or "delinquent") did occur in association with others, thus the notion of general learning theory is supported. However, Sutherland's (1939) theory of differential association is a most general theoretical perspective, since Sutherland himself indicates that differential association explains both routine, conventional behavior as well as "criminal" or "delinquent" behavior. Owing to the very general nature of this theory, and the fact that it was chosen because it provided background to the other theoretical perspectives, it will not be critiqued.

The first theoretical perspective to be commented on is subcultural theory as developed by Cohen (1955). This perspective can be critiqued on the basis of the findings from this study. Specifically, most of the research on subcultural theory seems to presuppose the existence of a "delinquent" subculture, and then seeks to identify the characteristics of that subculture. The findings of this study suggest that there is not necessarily a "delinquent" subculture (Cohen and Short, 1958). Rather, the findings suggest that members of various types (subcultures) of adolescents engaged in "delinquent" activities (e.g., drug use). Similarly, subcultural theory, as traditionally and originally developed, equates the delinquent subculture with the lower-class adolescent, specifically the lower-class male. Many of the studies that have utilized this theoretical perspective also accept the notion that the subculture consists of lower-class youth (usually male), and their findings tend to corroborate this assumption (e.g., Sugden and Yiannakis, 1982; Segrave and Chu, 1978). Another study (Levine and Kozak, 1979), however, also working within this general theoretical tradition (though not directly testing the theory), has concluded that there are no subcultural differences based upon class in terms of involvement in delinquency but rather that the peer group constitutes a subculture and that different peer groups have an effect upon delinquency. As far as drug use and the concept of subculture is concerned, the findings of McCann et al. (1977) support the notion of a "deviant" subculture based upon drug use. However, Huba et al. (1979), using quantitative methodology, rejected the idea of a single, general adolescent subculture and the existence of drug-specific subcultures. Thus, while several studies accept the theoretical concepts as developed, it can also be seen that the traditional notion of a delinquent subculture being equated with the lower class may be questionable at best, since other studies also indicate the existence of subcultures based upon other criteria (e.g., drug use, peer group, athletic involvement). The findings of this study attest to the fact that subcultures can be defined along dimensions other than that used to define a "delinquent" subculture, in relationship to membership in the lower social class. The critique noted here is basically that the original development of the concept of subculture, as put forth by Cohen (1955), is much too confining in scope and that refinements and reinterpretations of the concept of subculture (Donnelly, 1981b; Pearson, 1981; Shibutani, 1955; see earlier discussions in this chapter and in Chapter 2) seem appropriate in order that more workable conceptual, theoretical, and empirical endeavors may be undertaken.

In a related fashion, the findings of this study further suggest that the assumptions of subcultural theory concerning delinquents' "turning upside down the norms of the larger culture" are simply fallacious. The findings of this study show that adolescents (who by traditional standards may be defined as "delinquent" because of their drug use) in fact did not reject, or "turn upside down," the norms of the larger culture. It can be inferred, rather, that they simply were behaving in accord with one of a *multitude* of norms of the larger culture, and of their own adolescent subcultures. Drug use, especially use of alcohol and legitimate prescription drugs, is ubiquitous in the culture. That some adolescents use drugs may support the notion of a drug-using subculture (or perhaps subcultures — see Huba et al., 1979); or the presence of drug use in some other subcultures (e.g., athletes); or it may simply be evidence of the larger sociocultural pattern of drug use in the American society.

Turning attention to social control theories, specifically social control theory as developed by Hirschi (1969), several comments can be made. First, simply in terms of the development of the theory, Hirschi's empirical findings are based primarily on a group of white males. Similarly, the findings, suggesting the importance of the educational context in terms of "social bonding," and the complex path model of the social bond developed by Wiatrowski et al. (1981), were based on data from a sample of boys. This fact by itself needs to be kept in mind when attempting to utilize and generalize the theory to a sample of both females and males. It is possible that the same factors do not apply, or that they do not apply in the same ways, for females.[32]

The findings of Hindelang's (1973) replication of Hirschi's study, although conducted in a different geographic and demographic area, and including girls, in essence came to most of the same conclusions as Hirschi's original study. In the one area of difference (related to peer attachments), Hindelang suggested that Hirschi's theory "may need to be reconceptualized in terms of attachment to conventional and unconventional peers" (1973:487). This seems to be a most useful suggestion, although the problem of definition of "conventional" and "unconventional" still remains.

The findings of the current study help bring into focus a number of conceptual and theoretical problems within Hirschi's (1969) control theory, Hindelang's (1973) replication, and Wiatrowski et al.'s (1981) work:

1. A lack of conceptual clarity with regard to such terms as "bond to society," "weakening of social bonds," "conventional society," and the connection of these to delinquency. The findings of this study showed that even adolescents who were "bonded" to society through involvement in "conventional" activities (e.g., sports) still engaged in "delinquent" activities (i.e., drug use).

2. A major conceptual and theoretical weakness in the use of parental attachment as a measure of attachment when this concept is considered in relation to "normal" adolescent developmental tasks (see discussion, Chapter 2).

3. A problem with respect to the meaning of "the rules of society" (Hirschi, 1969:26) — whose rules and what rules? Does this mean legal statutes? Or "dominant social norms"? Or does it mean the rules set forth by one's parents and by teachers, coaches, and so on as specific representatives of the abstraction known as "society"? Or does this mean the rules of one's own "society"?

4. A conceptual dilemma with regard to the meaning of "conventional" activities (Gibbs, 1981) and "conformity." "Conventional" activities and what constitutes "conformity" vary by time, place and "culture." In this sense, adolescent drug use may be very "conventional" and very much evidence of "conformity" (e.g., use of drugs at a party; use of codeine to relieve pain in order to be able to continue playing one's sport).

5. A similar conceptual problem with the notion that the greater the stake in conformity, the less likely the individual is to maintain "delinquent" companions. The notion of "delinquent" companions may be a situationally defined concept, not a constant. For example, the findings of this study show that drug use is only one of many activities that occupy the social worlds

of the adolescents. "Delinquent" companions may be only those who share the actual drug-taking activities, and this label of "delinquent" companion may apply only at the time of the drug consumption. By the same token, these same individuals, when engaged in other types of activities, might not be seen as "delinquent." Similarly, companionship may be maintained for "delinquent" activity only, or may be maintained for a variety of types of activities. Likewise, (as was the case with subcultural theory), perhaps it would be more fruitful to formulate theory that deals with "delinquent" *activities* rather than "delinquent" persons, given the number of nondelinquent activities in which the adolescents also engage. (This would also avoid another problem inherent in the labeling process — that is, conferring a "master status" [Becker, 1963]).

6. Related to all of the foregoing is the finding of this study that even those adolescents who *are* "bonded" to society through "conventional" activities still engage in "deviant" and "delinquent" activities — in this case, drug use. Such findings are antithetical to Hirschi's claims.

In sum, Hirschi's control theory (1969), while an important contribution to the delinquency literature, is beset with major problems because of its inherent lack of conceptual clarity and the weakness of at least one of the prescribed elements of the "social bond" (i.e., parental attachment). Also, Hirschi's original study (1969), Hindelang's replication (1973), and Wiatrowski et al.'s (1981) use of control theory employed quantitative methodology, which, by design, limits the breadth and depth of information and explanations from the adolescents who are the subjects of the studies — information and rich explanations which can be obtained only from a qualitative study, such as this one.

Finally, as far as neutralization theory (Sykes and Matza, 1957) is concerned, the one major criticism that can be leveled revolves around the unanswered question of when the neutralization (justification, rationalization) occurs: before the commission of the act? during it? after the act is complete but before the actor is called upon to explain it? or at the time the actor is called upon to explain her/his behavior? This may be an unanswerable question at this point, and further research is needed to extend and clarify this theory. However, the findings of this study do support neutralization theory as currently conceived by Sykes and Matza (1957), and extend the work of Weinstein (1980), in that the data show that techniques of neutralization were very much in evidence when questions pertaining to their reasons for drug use/nonuse were asked of the adolescents.

CONCLUSION

This chapter has attempted to utilize the various theoretical perspectives presented in Chapter 2 to elucidate the empirical findings of this study and, conversely, to utilize the findings of this study in order to illuminate theory. The next chapter will summarize all of the foregoing chapters and will offer some specific policy recommendations based on the data.

NOTES

1.   However, it should be noted that for all but a few individuals, use of drugs (primarily alcohol and marijuana) was not defined by the adolescents themselves as "delinquent," "deviant," or as "abusive."

2.   The notion of "conventional" norms was criticized earlier in this study. However in keeping with the conceptualizations and findings of previous research, "conventional" was used to mean not using drugs, staying in school, aspiring to good jobs, and so on.

3.   It may be the case that media portrayals in the form of TV films, movies, docu-dramas, and the like, as well as educational films, provide information about drugs that causes youth to fear their effects. Of course, it is also possible that such mediated images, rather than influencing individuals in the direction of nonuse of drugs, may pique their curiosity, and possibly lead to trial and/or use of drugs. This appears to be a fruitful area for further research.

4.   It should be kept in mind that these studies included a variety of forms of "deviant" behavior (e.g., property, personal, minor, and drug "crimes"), not simply drug use.

5.   On a grander scale, all of the theoretical issues to be addressed in this chapter are also actually variants of learning theory, since each theory implies (or states) the learning of social and cultural values and expectations. For example, if one is "bonded" to society (Hirschi, 1969), one certainly has learned and accepted the values of the society. Likewise, if one must use neutralization techniques because one cannot be "totally immune from the demands for conformity made by the dominant social order" (Sykes and Matza, 1957:665), then it follows that one has already learned what those demands are.

6.   "Delinquent" is put in quotes to emphasize the fact that application of the label of "delinquent" is dependent, not upon the fact or act of drug use, but upon the one who is doing the labeling. The adolescents in this study do not define their drug use as "delinquent," although it is traditionally categorized as such.

7.   This *may* be an artifact of sampling bias since school district lists were used in the larger sampling procedure.

8.   Several of the athletes spoke specifically of drug problems and drug use among professional athletes. These youth indicated that they believed that it was because

athletes made a lot of money that they could and did do drugs; they also believed that team physicians provided drugs to players.

9.   The idea of subculture within sociological literature usually refers to "deviant" groups and activities, often gang behavior (cf., Rubington and Weinberg, 1981; Cloward and Ohlin, 1960; Kitsuse and Dietrick, 1959; Cohen, 1955). It is critical to know who is doing the labeling of "deviant" and what is meant by the term, for the adolescents in this study who smoked and drank gave no evidence that, according to the norms of their social worlds, they in any way perceived themselves as "deviant."

10.   However, the unanswered question is how small or large a group is a subculture, and what precisely characterizes a subculture. Explanations of this question could constitute an entire study itself.

11.   One of the difficulties of using Hirschi's theory is that the meaning of the term "bond" is unclear. For purposes of this study, "bond" will refer to evidence (behavioral and verbal) of the individual's apparent acceptance of (or at least learning of) typical social values, norms, and expectations learned through membership and socialization in her/his various social groups and institutions (e.g., family, church, school, sports groups, peer groups, the society as a whole).

12.   It would seem that another problem with Hirschi's theoretical development is the apparent inseparable relationship between the elements of attachment and belief and between those of commitment and involvement. Hirschi relates them so often that it is difficult to deal separately with the elements, yet for theoretical purposes he separated them.

13.   Once again, the term "delinquency" is used by theorists to include a variety of activities, including drug use. Keep in mind the essence of notes 1 and 5, and remember that the adolescents do not necessarily define drug use as "delinquent."

14.   Hirschi's work does not explain *how* the social bond becomes "weakened" or precisely what that means, other than to speak of the consequences of that weakening (i.e., delinquency).

15.   This observation is based upon a comparison of percentages of individuals reporting involvement with sports and percentages of individuals reporting involvement with drugs. No regression, correlation, or other statistical tests were performed, nor are these implied.

16.   Again, note 5 is important. Within the examination of these theoretical perspectives, there is an implied acceptance of the term "delinquent" and "delinquency" as traditionally used by researchers. Whether the substance use engaged in by the adolescents in this study is seen *by them* as delinquent is an entirely different question. It can be speculated that, in fact, most do not see substance use as a type of delinquent activity, for they do not call themselves by any names which imply delinquency and, in fact, accept the use of alcohol and other drugs as routine events in their lives.

17.   Nonathletes may also engage in more "other" delinquency (e.g., crime). Although this is not investigated in this study, the notion that more nonathletes are involved in delinquency is supported by much research (Segrave and Hastad, 1982; Buhrman and Bratton, 1978; Landers and Landers, 1977; Segrave and Chu, 1978; Buhrman, 1977; Landers, 1976; Schafer, 1969a, 1969b).

18.   Of course, there would still be conceptual dilemmas, for example, just what did Hirschi mean by "weakening bonds"? What would be meant by "conventional" society, and the theoretical problems mentioned above — that is, individuals who apparently are "bonded" to "conventional" society and who engage in traditionally

"delinquent" behaviors like drug use? Perhaps one of the major conceptual and theoretical issues to note here is the need to heed Mills' (1959) contribution concerning the intersection of biography and history at a point in a given culture, and recognize that perhaps drug use, especially in this age group and of the type observed most frequently (e.g., alcohol and marijuana) *is or may be* quite "conventional" behavior.

19.   A question can be raised concerning "delinquent" activities engaged in by these and other adolescents and the socio-cultural "expectations" that "boys will be boys," "kids will be kids." Even though some segments and agents of society view the drinking of alcohol by those under age and/or by youthful athletes, and the taking of other kinds of drugs by anyone, as "delinquent" or illegal, a moratorium on the expectations concerning drinking and drug taking (perhaps only experimentation with "light" drugs) is expressed in the socio-cultural "expectations" that "boys will be boys"; thus, drinking and cigarette smoking and light drug experimentation are thought by some "to be expected" by youth and in this sense are not seen as "delinquent." This type of socio-cultural "mixed message" needs further investigation.

20.   In describing denial of injury, Sykes and Matza (1957:667) state that this concept "turn[s] on the question of whether or not anyone has clearly been hurt by [the] deviance, and this matter is open to a variety of interpretations." In their discussion, Sykes and Matza (and others using this technique) all seem to imply that the injury occurs to someone other than the "delinquent" actor, or something that belongs to others than the "delinquent" actor. While this may be the traditional sense in which denial of injury has been interpreted, since Sykes and Matza themselves indicate that the issue of anyone's being hurt is open to interpretation, it seems perfectly legitimate to interpret denial of injury to include denial of injury to oneself (and in this case, actually aiding, or enhancing one's performance).

21.   These various loci of authority also are evidence of the fact that adolescents belong to a multiplicity of subcultures.

22.   For example, the use of alcohol and other drugs by athletes on the weekends during the sport season, and at any time during the off season, seemed to indicate that the norms of drug-using peers took precedence over the norms of athletics concerning training and care of the body at these times. Likewise, the use of certain drugs for specific sport-related reasons also reflected a situationally defined loyalty — giving the best to the team being of primary concern.

23.   See note 21.

24.   The explanations given by youth very much parallel reasons offered by adults in the "society at large." Thus, owing to the notion of a pluralistic society and norm multiplicity, *some* segments of society may accept as valid some of these adolescent explanations for drug use.

25.   Related to this, Mitchell and Dodder (1983) found that neutralization was a salient predictor of what they called "minor delinquency" (i.e., getting drunk, driving without a license, truancy, disobeying parents).

26.   Condemnation of the condemners, also a technique of neutralization, was also mentioned, though not nearly so often as the other two techniques. In fact, as far as drug use was concerned, this particular technique of neutralization was mentioned quite frequently in discussions of cigarette smoking (not a topic of concern to this study), though not nearly so often in regard to other drugs.

27.   Mitchell and Dodder's (1983) study included forms of delinquency other than drug use. Hence, as with other studies, the difference in findings may be due to this fact.

28.   Related to the fourth claim above, many of the nonusers gave as a reason for nonuse of drugs the illegality or "wrongness" of substance use. This is perhaps suggestive of the fact that neutralization techniques might allow these particular youth to "disclaim wrongdoing" and thus to use drugs. Again, this appears to be evidence that not only must the delinquency and the techniques be examined but also the actor her/himself in order to better understand "delinquency."

29.   It must be kept in mind that while such behaviors may be seen as "delinquent" vis-à-vis the expectations of the dominant culture, the youth who so behave are very much conforming to the norms of their respective subgroups' loci of authority.

30.   Again, females most often gave as a reason for lack of involvement in sports that activity was "boring and tiring."

31.   The same criticism can be made of research in many areas both within and outside of sociology. For example, within psychology, Kohlberg's (1981) findings related to moral development, based upon studies of only males, has been much discussed (Gilligan, 1982). (See also Belenkey et al., 1986; Andersen, 1983; Stanley and Wise, 1983, for commentary on the general topic of the use of male subjects and generalization to all people.)

32.   Despite this observation, this author obviously did use Hirschi's theory (1969) as it stands. Since this was not a study of gender differences specifically, and since there were, in fact, few differences between girls and boys in this sample, especially in terms of their explanations for drug use/nonuse, this issue was not viewed as critical. However, if this study had focused specifically upon the exploration of gender differences, this observation might have produced greater concern.

7

Summary and
Policy Recommendations

The preceding chapters have discussed the various questions of empirical and theoretical interest in this study. The evidence has suggested that there are no marked differences between athletes and nonathletes in their explanations of drug use/nonuse, and that for some individuals, sports are very important in their lives, yet for others, sports are not even mentioned in their discussions. As far as other aspects of the study are concerned, the findings are much more complex: Some adolescents who are involved in sports actively used alcohol and other drugs, some specifically for purposes related to sports performance; other youth specifically chose sports involvement and/or athletic peers as a way of preventing or tempering drug use. Related to this, the evidence supports the contention that sport is an institution with its own values, beliefs, and norms, and is an agent of social control. At the same time, the evidence also indicated that *different* sets of norms, values, and beliefs exist within the institution of sport.

The quest for clear, simple policy implications from any research is at best naïve. The search for simplistic, one-dimensional policy recommendations from this study is definitely fruitless, for the findings of this study, both theoretically and empirically, reflect the multiplicity and complexity of the social worlds of the adolescents in this study, and by extension, of adolescents in general.

SUMMARY AND RECOMMENDATIONS

General

Initially, the findings of this study indicated that the social worlds of the youth in this study were not appreciably different: Athletes and nonathletes differed primarily by virtue of the sports involvement of those designated as athletes. Regardless of classification concerning sports participation or drug use, the youth were almost all in school; all but a few claimed membership in some religious denomination (even if they did not actively practice); nearly all indicated that having and spending time with friends was very important; most envisioned having jobs, usually well-paying, in their futures. Since there has been practically no other research that has focused upon the similarities and differences between drug users and nonusers in terms of their larger social worlds, not simply in terms of use or nonuse of drugs, it seemed important to investigate the larger picture in an attempt to begin to learn what factors affect substance use and nonuse, including the changing nature of society (Bedworth, 1971). Thus, the first recommendation:

RECOMMENDATION 1: There needs to be more research conducted that investigates the world of adolescents in an attempt to determine in what ways adolescents, both drug using and nonusing, are alike and in what ways they are different.

Drugs: Use and Nonuse — Knowledge and Prevention

When the issue of drug use was examined, in general there were similarities (as well as differences) among all the adolescents in terms of the reasons for use/nonuse of drugs. Over 60 percent of the adolescents were users of beer and/or liquor; 55 percent were users of marijuana; 27 percent were users of various hard drugs. However, it should be noted that for all but a few individuals, use of drugs (primarily alcohol and marijuana) was *not* defined by the adolescents themselves as "delin-quent," "deviant," or "abusive."

It is important to learn about the subjective meaning of drug use/ nonuse from the adolescents themselves, for without such knowledge it is very difficult to design alternative and/or prevention and rehabilita-tion programs that will be meaningful. While the worlds of the adult researcher and the adolescent drug user/nonuser are in some respects alike, in other ways those worlds may be very different. Thus, the second recommendation:

RECOMMENDATION 2: There needs to be more research conducted that seeks to obtain information from adolescents *about their drug-taking behaviors and* their *definitions and meanings of such, in an attempt to gather data free (if possible) of researcher bias concerning what is "abuse" and what, to adolescents, is "use."*

Reasons for Use. The reasons articulated for drug use by those individuals who used drugs were varied and included: physical effects (i.e., taste, sleep facilitation, enhancement, energy), mental and emotional effects (i.e., to get in a "good mood," to get "mellow"), specific effects (i.e., getting high or drunk), and for "fun"; "environmental" factors (i.e., general availability, availability at parties); and "motivational" reasons (i.e., simply wanting to, out of boredom). It *appears* from the reasons given for substance use that some individuals who used drugs were lacking stimulation and alternative activities, activities to replace the need for a chemical "high." The recommendation related to reasons for use follows the next section on the peer group.

The Peer Group

Related to the immediately foregoing is the role of the peer group in the lives of these adolescents. The findings of this study show that in almost all cases there was a similarity between the adolescent's peer group's use/nonuse and the adolescent's own use/nonuse of a given substance. For example, if an individual was a regular user of beer, most of her/his peer group were also regular users; if an individual was a nonuser, most of her/his peer group were also nonusers. Similarly, the findings also reveal that several youth deliberately changed peer groups to increase substance use, and a few others consciously changed peer groups in order to cut down, eliminate, or prevent their own involvement with drugs.

Research has shown that peer programs (sometimes called peer pressure programs) promote:

1. Greater sense of acceptance by peers
2. Greater pursuit and use of information provided by peers
3. Higher motivation to succeed in school
4. Greater willingness to express ideas to classmates

5. Higher achievement in a variety of academic tasks

6. Greater ability to understand the perspective of others

7. Higher self-esteem

8. More positive interpersonal relationships with school peers

9. More positive perception of and liking of school peers and school personnel (Johnson, 1980; Chase, 1981; Resnik and Gibbs, 1981:83).

Varenhorst (1981:17) cites the following more general, and more encompassing, benefits that can result from the development of various types of adolescent activity and peer programs:

1. Increased respect from adults, for participating, contributing, being responsible, worthy members of the community and of society.

2. Increased time and involvement from adults, and more qualified youth leaders (e.g., as in the Big Brother/Big Sister programs; providing role models, and respect and love for youth).

3. Constructive opportunities to be actively involved with the life of the community (e.g., voluntarism, part- or full-time employment, etc.).

4. Help in developing social competence (e.g., how to care for another person, how to be a friend).

5. Opportunities for moral development and to explore the meaning of life for oneself with one's peers. (See also Johnson et al., 1986; Chase, 1981; Gaus, 1981.)

In light of these suggestions from the literature and the findings of this study pertaining both to the peer group and to reasons for use the following recommendation is set forth:

RECOMMENDATION 3: Develop new and enhance existing peer programs, not simply to address the delinquent youth, but to provide all youth with positive activities in which to engage. Such positive, alternative activities should provide activities so that the youth are not bored, and provide stimulation so that an additional "high" is not sought through drugs.

Health Education

Adolescents who did not use marijuana (51%) gave several types of reasons for their nonuse: generalized, nonspecific fear (e.g., being "scared"), fear of harming one's body (e.g., cancer), fear of addiction. For nonusers of beer (32%) and liquor (39%), the explanations included: fear of loss of control, fear of effects on the body (e.g., "sloppy, falling down"; "eats up your insides"; getting sick). Nonusers of hard drugs (79%) offered the following explanations: generalized fear (e.g., "freakin' out," "gettin' messed up"), fear of harming one's body (e.g., "harming your organs," death), fear of addiction (see Haines, 1983; Segal et al., 1983).

Most of the adolescents indicated that they learned about drugs and alcohol and their effects (and thus their fears) from health classes. While educational programming may not work for all youth or all people, the data indicate that indeed the lessons, films, discussions, and the like from health education classes were sources of information that caused many adolescents to temper their use of drugs. In fact, "fear" tactics of presentation, criticized by some and supported by others (see Pickens, 1985; Williams et al., 1985; Haines, 1983; Antonow et al., 1976; Fritzen and Mazer, 1975; Mathews, 1975, for discussions of fear tactics in educational endeavors), seemed effective for some of the youth (e.g., many expressed fears of becoming "junkies" or addicts and fear of using needles, based upon films seen in health classes). Related to these findings are the following:

RECOMMENDATION 4: Maintain and expand health education efforts, focused upon youth and the general public, both in the schools and through community health programs.

Additionally,

RECOMMENDATION 5: Assertiveness training should be included in the health education curriculum so that youth may develop the skills that will enable them to resist pressure from peers encouraging them to try various substances or to engage in other types of "delinquent" behaviors (LeMonn, 1987; Resnik and Gibbs, 1981).

Rather than simply maintaining health education programs, typically offered in junior and senior high school classes, the data also support the need to start such education earlier or expand existing elementary health education programs.[1]

Drugs: Use and Treatment

The data cited earlier indicate what is already known: American youth are using alcohol and drugs. If agents of social control continue to see such use as "delinquent" or "deviant," and if there continue to be the assumption and practice of somehow "treating" youths who use (and abuse, however this is defined) these substances, then several recommendations seem appropriate:

RECOMMENDATION 6: Conduct research pertaining to the effectiveness — positive, pro-social effectiveness — of such traditional "treatment" for juveniles as placing them in detention facilities.

If Sutherland's theory of differential association is valid, and research seems to indicate that it is, placing youths who have somehow violated social norms and/or legal statutes together in the same facility, isolated from non–norm-violating individuals seems merely to facilitate the interaction of individuals who already are predisposed to "delinquency," at least by social control agents' labeling of them as such.[2] This leads to several additional recommendations:

RECOMMENDATION 7: Commitment of time, energy, person-power, and money is needed to devise alternative arrangements for "youthful offenders." This is especially important if the findings of such research, as is suggested in Recommendation 6, indicate that, in fact, the criminal-juvenile justice system is indeed facilitating differential association of individuals disposed to "delinquent" activities by isolating them in detention facilities.

RECOMMENDATION 8: As an alternative, establish a "peer-buddy" system or program, similar to the Big Brother/Big Sister program, to assist with drug "rehabilitation" and treatment.[3]

If the theoretical tenets of differential association are accepted, it would make sense to attempt to have "delinquent" youths differentially associate with nondelinquent peers, in an attempt to have the "delinquent" learn some of the values and beliefs of the nondelinquent youths (Norem-Hebeisen and Hedin, 1981; Resnik and Gibbs, 1981).[4]

If one accepts the premises of Matza's neutralization theory, then this recommendation should not appear quite so impossible as it might otherwise. If delinquent youths still have and hold to "conventional" norms and expectations, then pairing them with nondelinquent youths is not necessarily an attempt to have them learn *new* values, beliefs, and so on, but rather is an attempt to rekindle and reinforce already existent, but temporarily neutralized, norms and beliefs.

Sports Participation

Sports participation was an important part of the lives of many of the youth in this study: 69 percent of the boys and 45 percent of the girls were classified as athletes in this study. For these youth, sports were an activity in which they spent time generally, leaving little free time in which to get bored; and sports were a vehicle for spending time with friends. Likewise, for many of these youth (nearly all male), sports were a life goal of some sort.

On another level, in terms of substance use, the athletic peer group was one specific peer group to which adolescents changed when they wished an alternative to substance use. For other youth, it was not only the athletic peer group which served as a deterrent or alternative to drug use; many of the adolescents indicated that it was specifically their own personal involvement in sports programs that helped them limit or prevent drug use.

For some of the youth so involved, athletic activity (either organized sports or activities in physical education class) was an important factor as far as school was concerned: physical education was often mentioned as the favorite school subject of youth; participation on a sports team was given as a reason to stay in school or to refrain from being truant. In view of these findings, the following is offered:

RECOMMENDATION 9: Reinstate and increase program offerings in physical education and athletics for boys and girls at the elementary, junior high, and senior high school levels.

In fact, Resnik and Gibbs (1981:51) comment that "natural groupings such as social cliques and commonly recognizable types," including "jocks," provide a logical setting for peer-oriented delinquency prevention programs. If sports are a reason for some to remain in school, and if it is felt that school has something to offer adolescents, then it would seem that any class or activity that helps keep adolescents in school ought to be supported and reinforced.

Physical education classes, sports programs, and athletic programs should allow more adolescents to participate regularly and actively so that perhaps more youth (*both* girls and boys) would become physically active. Through such activity, perhaps adolescents would become more "bonded" to school and to society, and thus might engage in fewer "delinquent" activities.

Related to this, when asked about their favorite subject in school, for some of the youth, physical education was the answer — again, a reason why they have stayed in school. However, among both those who like physical education or sports and claimed that it was the reason for their staying in school and those who did not like these activities, there was a criticism that the activities often were "boring" and repetitious. Here then is a policy recommendation within a recommendation:

RECOMMENDATION 9a: Reexamine and revise the curricula that exist in physical education; alternative, challenging activities, as well as instruction in popular team sports (i.e., basketball, volleyball, softball, baseball, soccer, etc.) are needed in order for students to feel interested and motivated.

Implicit in this recommendation is a need for (1) more variety; (2) more progressive instruction and development of skill levels (so that, for example, for four or more years of physical education classes in which basketball is taught, students do not remain at basically the same level of play, with little or no attention to increasing skill development); (3) more offerings in individual and life-time sports (e.g., bowling, tennis, golf, skating, etc.), which are more likely to be played when the school years are over, since these activities can be done alone or with one other person, rather than with an entire team; (4) the inclusion of programs such as Outward Bound, ropes courses, rock climbing, and the like, since research has shown that such programs are much more successful than conventional physical activities for "delinquency"-prone individuals (Wichmann, 1983; Chase, 1981; Gaus, 1981; Sugden and Yiannakis, 1982; Baer, Jacobs, and Carr, 1975; Kelly and Baer, 1971; Lee and Schroder, 1969).

Along with expansion and retention of athletic programs, attention needs to be paid to enforcing policies regarding: (1) requirements for school attendance and athletic participation — establishing expectations and requirements that may "force" adolescents to stay in school in order to participate in sports programs; (2) the objectives of the sports and athletics programs. These objectives should include:

1. Educational goals, as well as competitive outcomes, so that positive learning may occur within the context of the sports program as well as within the larger school setting.
2. Opportunity to play for the fun of it and to develop skill, rather than simply winning, through utilizing only the "best" players.
3. Co-curricular objectives that coincide with the school's other educational and societal objectives.[5]

Without attention to the above, sport may be viewed as an end in itself, and not a mechanism for positive social learning and bonding. Thus,

RECOMMENDATION 10: Faculty, administration, and school boards should continuously examine policy and objectives relative to the athletic and sports programs. This means, for example, that for interscholastic varsity play, (a) broader and more abstract educational objectives are sought; (b) eligibility requirements are established and/or carefully adhered to; (c) cuts from teams are done fairly; (d) training rules are uniformly applied to all who may break them; (e) equal treatment for violations of school policy and societal expectations is afforded both athletes and nonathletes — that is, no special dispensations for athletes.

If it is believed that sports and athletics are agents of socialization and of social control, then programs for *all* children and youth must be developed, allowing all to participate and learn from all types of sports, not simply the boys and/or the best in the "major" sports (i.e., baseball, boys' basketball, football).[6]

If it is believed that there are rules that make a sport a sport, and if there are rules pertaining to training and conduct for any athlete, then a new commitment to those rules seems to be in order. A coach telling players to "break heads or bones," or a coach teaching illegal moves, is clearly teaching "delinquent," "deviant" lessons vis-à-vis the established rules of the game. Similarly, if there exist training rules regarding such activities as drug use, but at the same time "legitimate" drugs are provided in order that young athletes can play (allegedly) better or without pain, then a mixed message is being conveyed to youth, a message that very well may help to legitimize other forms of drug use (for which the youth will be called "delinquent" if caught; and which is generally called "delinquent" by the powers that be).

The double standard and the tendency to "turn the other way" when an athlete, particularly a star athlete, is caught breaking training rules (e.g., drinking, smoking, or taking drugs) or when athletes have been caught engaging in some form of "delinquency" (e.g., vandalism, violence against others, intimidation, property damage, etc.) serve only to weaken the pro-social values that sports can and do, theoretically, teach and to weaken the social control functions ostensibly served by sports involvement. The "turning the other way" sanctions the adolescents' involvement in "delinquent" activities, often under the social justification that "boys will be boys," a justification held not only by coaches but by segments of the general public as well.[7] Thus,

RECOMMENDATION 11: Schools, colleges, and universities as well as sports governing bodies must develop or expand training programs for coaches that emphasize ethics and fair play as well as the problems and dangers of "legal" drugs prescribed for use by players and the need for uniform application of and attention to expectations.

RECOMMENDATION 12: All social structures and social actors — schools, churches and synagogues, the media, the social control agents (e.g., parents, teachers, coaches, reporters, etc.) — must carefully examine and strive to eliminate from society's institutions and agencies the double standards related to sports, athletics, rules and regulations, and "delinquency" in general. Such double standards not only demean the ideals of sports, but also teach lessons about survival in the social world that undermine the ideal norms and values which sports and other institutions are attempting to instill in youth.

The School

Related in some ways to the above, many of the youth in this study found school to be "boring." If school is boring, then students are apt to have time to kill and may find themselves with opportunities to engage in "deviant" or "delinquent" behaviors, perhaps simply because they are "bored" and "have nothing to do." From this observation comes this recommendation:

RECOMMENDATION 13: Curricular issues within the school as a whole need to be examined. More challenging, more individualized offerings need to be made available to students.[8]

The Larger Social World: The Community

Policy recommendations for the community parallel many of the recommendations just given, since there is (or ought to be) cooperation and a good working relationship between the school and the community. Since the worlds of the adolescents presented in this study do not exist in a research vacuum, but in fact are embedded in the larger world of which they are a part, these recommendations are important.

RECOMMENDATION 14: Expand existing athletic and sports programs within the community and develop new athletic opportunities for youth.[9]

Role Models in the Larger Community. Role models exist everywhere in society, for youth and others alike; it is important to attend to what is being modeled. In terms of sport and sports figures, Research & Forecasts (1983:62–63) found, in a nationwide study, that 75 percent of the American public considered athletes to be good role models for children, and 59 percent agreed that athletes are the *best* role models children can have. If this is the belief of the American public, then attention needs to be paid to the amount and kind of media portrayal given to athletes. The reports of drug scandals in professional sports, the articles dealing with drug use by Olympic athletes, the various articles and letters to editors concerning drug use by local athletes (usually high school) — all present media images that show athletics and drugs going hand-in-hand, certainly a mixed message given the research findings cited previously (Adams and Resnik, 1985).[10]

If there is a concern about youthful drinking, for example, one need look no further than the TV, radio, newspapers, news magazines, and the home and neighborhood to see the socialization messages concerning alcohol consumption. Drinking is portrayed as glamorous and "adult," and no social gathering can take place without it (*New York Times,* May 26, 1985).

If there is concern about youthful use of other drugs, again one must look at the mediated images. Videos and movies portraying hard drug use abound. Sheppard (1980) and Adler and Lotecka (1973) found that mass media were very important influences on use and perceived credibility of drug information. For habitual users, the media were second only to drug-using peers as an information source. (See also U.S. Senate Committee on Governmental Affairs, 1985.)

Additionally, if there is concern about youthful use of other drugs, one must look around the home. The medicine cabinet is full of drugs, prescription and nonprescription, prescribed for and taken to deal with "the human problems of living." For more and more people, drugs "hold out the promise of instant relief for psychological pains" (Hills, 1980:127). Indeed, it appears that the whole medical industry has been engaged in a concerted effort to persuade "the public that *unpleasant human feelings are abnormal* — an 'illness' that should be corrected with drugs," as a result of which "chemical alteration of human consciousness is becoming a fact of life" (Hills, 1980:118, 135).[11]

If there is concern about youthful vandalism, property destruction, and violence, again one must look at the larger social world and its role models and the media. This culture venerates violence and destruction, in books, films, TV programs, and news stories (Barlow, 1984:131).

The following recommendations, based upon the foregoing, are a bit more ambitious in that they address larger structural issues and social facts in need of attention, and of great importance.

RECOMMENDATION 15: Attend to the images and role models that the larger society provides, particularly in the area of substance use, especially as these are broadcast and enhanced by the media.

Shared Responsibility in the Larger Community. As is usually the case when there is a "social problem," a typical characterization of "delinquency," the focus of attention is almost exclusively on the perpetrator. Young people are part of the world; they are not simply individuals held in abeyance somewhere along the developmental scale. As such, their problems are societal problems, and the solutions must be broader based societal solutions (Lohrmann and Fors, 1986), not a victim-blame approach (Ryan, 1976). Little attention has been paid to the social structures, conventions, expectations, and hypocrisies that play a part in an individual's "delinquency." By this it is not meant that individuals are not responsible for their actions, but rather that they are probably not the *only* ones responsible for the conditions and situations that have led to the "delinquency."[12]

Schools whose curricula cannot hold the attention of students also share the blame. Coaches who teach young people (typically males) how to "break bones or heads"; coaches, teachers, and parents who look the other way while the youths, athletes, and others engage in acts of vandalism, intimidation, property damage, excesses in drinking, and the like, under the familiar social justification of "boys (and sometimes girls) will be boys" share responsibility. All social actors who convey "mixed messages" to youth regarding various behaviors (e.g., a parent who drinks regularly while telling a child not to drink; a parent with a cigarette dangling out of her/his mouth or with a beer in hand, at the same time instructing that child on the evils of smoking and/or drinking and indicating proscriptions against such activities [Anderson, 1971]) must also be held accountable. The media that reinforce stereotypes and glamorize violence, destruction, or drinking must likewise share the responsibility. All these are social actors and social facts that impinge on youth. We must not simply look at the youth as the ones in need of treatment, rehabilitation, detention, incarceration, and so on. Indeed,

There is no drug abuse problem, only a people problem. Young people need an alternative to drugs and this alternative cannot be found unless parents are willing to change both their drinking and drug abuse habits. The answer to the drug problem must be found not in pharmacology but at the grass roots level, on a one-to-one basis and the problem must be treated as an overall mental health problem (Anderson, 1971:391).

Thus,

RECOMMENDATION 16: Shift away from a "victim blame" mentality to an examination of the interactions of all segments of society in producing the "problem adolescent," the "delinquent."

The Iran-Contra affair, the Watergate episode, the Vietnam War, and other governmental transgressions and double standards of various enforcement agencies have led to a rather pervasive distrust of authority figures and a questioning of that authority and the application of rules and sanctions emanating from these agents of social control (Simon and Eitzen, 1982). Such double standards are not only evident at the highest levels of governmental and corporate activities but are also apparent in the daily lives of everyone, including the adolescents in this study.

The remedy for adolescent transgressions, including drug use, lies not simply with the adolescents, but with all of us.

NOTES

1. While not a usage written about in this document, many youth in this study claim to have started smoking cigarettes as young as 8 or 9 years of age. Similarly, for some of these individuals, marijuana and alcohol use was begun at 9 or 10 years of age.

2. While not a theory utilized in this study, labeling theory posits that official labeling of an individual, with its attendant stigmatization, might very well facilitate the individual's transition to secondary or career deviance. If isolating adolescents in detention facilities with the concomitant labeling of "youthful offenders" is often standard practice, it seems evident that research is needed to determine if this practice, along with the differential association that must take place in such facilities, is in fact leading to these adolescents' continuing involvement in delinquent or criminal behaviors.

3. Obviously, this particular suggestion also has some potential problems in terms of implementation: Persons under the age of majority whose parents might not want them associated with officially labeled "delinquent" youths, nondelinquent youths who themselves might not want anything to do with "delinquents," the question of whether or not positive, pro-social values of the nondelinquent youths can be transmitted to the "delinquents," or whether friendships or the peer relationships can be formed by programs that might "artificially" bring adolescents together.

4. Of course, there is also the risk that nondelinquent adolescents will also learn some of the values, beliefs, and so on of the "delinquent" youth!

5. The school's educational objectives (motivating students to learn, preparing for adulthood, "trying to be one's best," equality, etc.) are contrasted with the objectives of the "hidden curriculum" (e.g., winning as the most important goal; looking the other way if players violate training and/or other school expectations and rules, especially if the players are "stars," vital to a victory), which do not reflect the ideal in terms of educational objectives.

6. This would address the double standard in relation to gender involvement in sports and to the distinctions in terms of money, publicity, and the like made between "minor" and "major" sports.

7. In a community only thirty miles from the study community, during the spring of 1985, a heated debate took place in the local paper over just such issues, when some members of the high school wrestling team were suspended for drinking at a party (those who admitted it) and others were not so punished. However, many of those who wrote letters to the editor felt that there should have been no punishment at all, since "boys will be boys" and it occurred during a holiday period.

Similar editorial columns have appeared in 1985–1990 concerning the treatment of athletes at a nearby private university known for its basketball and football programs.

8. Implicit in this recommendation are a variety of constraints that need to be recognized, including: the nature of the educational bureaucracy, teacher salaries, teacher preparation, classroom size, and equipment needs.

9. As one subject in this study observed, if he had had an opportunity to be involved in some type of community recreation program, he would not have got himself into trouble.

10. Several of the subjects in the study, in fact, talked at great length about the use of drugs by professional athletes. Many of these youth felt that such use was "OK," either because the players made enough money to afford the substances or because the youth believed that team physicians prescribed or provided the drugs.

11. The use of licit drugs is the strongest indicator of the probability of the abuse of licit drugs and the use of illicit drugs (Barlow, 1984).

12. This does not mean the recent, and rather simplistic, practice adopted by some states of holding the parents responsible for the "delinquent" activities of their children.

8

Epilogue

The findings of this study include the following: Specifically, there were no marked differences between athletes and nonathletes in their explanations of drug use/nonuse. For some individuals, sports were very important in their lives; for others, sports were not even mentioned in their discussions. Some adolescents involved in sports actively and consciously used alcohol and other drugs, some specifically for purposes related to sports performance; other youth specifically chose sports involvement and/or athletic peers as a way of preventing or tempering drug use. In general, the social worlds of the adolescents in this study were not noticeably different. Participants and nonparticipants in sports did not talk about their activities differently, nor were there differences in the types of activities engaged in by the youth, the two exceptions being involvement in sports for those so involved and the more sedentary activities mentioned by the girls as ways they spent their time.

As far as general patterns in the rationalizations and explanations offered for drug use, there did not appear to be noticeable distinctions between participants and nonparticipants in sports, except in those instances where a drug was used for sport-specific purposes. In terms of rationalizations and explanations for nonuse of drugs, again there did not appear to be differences in major patterns of explanations between participants and nonparticipants in sports, although one minor pattern did appear. For some of the athletes, nonuse of drugs was explained in terms of concern for health and concern for the body.

Perhaps the finding of most consequence in this entire study is that the myth of "clean living" and sports was indeed held by the adolescents in this study. The majority of youth did seem to believe that "jocks" and "druggies" (i.e., those individuals who use drugs) were in fact separate groups and different kinds of people. This is an interesting contrast to another major finding of the study that many athletes use drugs. It is evidence of the *pervasiveness* and *success* of the use of various neutralization techniques that in essence allow the youth to believe the myth of sports and "clean living" (e.g., nonuse of drugs), at the same time that many of these individuals themselves *used* drugs *and* participated in sports. The belief in the marriage of sports and "clean living" held by these youth parallels the larger society's belief in the same myth (Research & Forecasts, 1983).

Another finding of significance (although this involved only a few athletes in this study) related especially to the statements immediately above is the apparently unquestioned acceptance of the practice of using specific hard drugs (e.g., codeine and "speed") for sport-related purposes and effects. This finding is significant because of its relation to Wiseman's (1974:326) concern regarding findings which "reveal[s] something of a more general (and significant) nature about human behavior." Because of the pervasiveness of drug use for sport-specific purposes in the larger society and in collegiate and professional sports, this finding should not be surprising. On the other hand, it is significant here because of the ease with which this rationalization and justification was offered by the youth engaged in this type of drug use.

As stated earlier, the quest for simplistic, one-dimensional policy recommendations from this, or any research, is at best naïve. The findings of this study, both theoretically and empirically, reflect the *multiplicity* and *complexity* of the social world of the adolescents in this study, and by extension of adolescents in general. The policy recommendations in the previous chapter address the complexity of this study by covering each of the dimensions of the findings.

In general, this research is also an addition to sociological knowledge for several reasons. First, it has provided extensive commentary and criticism of the various theories used, pointing out their strengths and weaknesses. Second, this research has extended previous empirical studies in that it dealt with the question of drug usage among adolescents who happened to be athletes, an area in which virtually no qualitative research within the sociology of sport (or within the area of substance use) had been done. Third, this study specifically extended the work of Sykes and Matza (1957) and Weinstein (1980) by illustrating neutralization theory specifically as exemplified in explanations of adolescent drug use. Fourth, this study contributed methodologically to the body of knowledge through its utilization of ethnographic techniques: participant observation and in-depth interviews. This is in contrast to much of the research in the area of adolescent drug use, which has used survey instruments that, with forced-choice answer categories, could only scratch the surface of drug use. Fifth, also methodologically, this study illustrated the capabilities for extensive use of the microcomputer, coupled with data management software, for analysis of ethnographic data. Sixth, the findings of this study are phenomenological in that the data presented utilized the words of the adolescents themselves — again, a contrast with previous studies, since little or no work has dealt with the way in which adolescents talk about (i.e., explain, justify, account for) drug usage. If social scientists and policymakers concerned with adolescents wish to produce work that can have a positive impact, the meaning of drug activity to youth as talked about by these youth is extremely important, for that meaning may be quite different from how the "experts" define it, not only because they each belong to different speech communities (Scott and Lyman, 1968) but also because:

All scientific explanations of the social world can, and for certain purposes must, refer to the subjective meaning of the actions of human beings from which social reality originates (Schutz, 1962:62).

Appendix:
Yule City Methodology

Yule City is a medium-size city of approximately 200,000 population in the northeastern United States, having demographic characteristics that approximate the national norms.[1] While no single area can be truly representative of the nation, this site offers a statistical profile that does not appear to depart significantly from that of New York State or the nation. That is, Yule City has a mean demographic profile for such variables as ethnic group diversity, income and education levels, crime rates, and life-styles.[2]

In order to make the study feasible, one quadrant of Yule City was examined very closely. Information about possible target areas was obtained from city officials, with special help from the superintendent of schools. An area of about six square miles, a quadrant which appeared most representative of the city, was the site for the majority of the data gathering. This area was chosen because local statistical profiles showed that the adolescents within this area came from every social class, from many ethnic groups (including about 25% blacks), and lived in a variety of housing and family situations; youths in the study area exhibited involvement in a wide range of delinquent activities. Within the data-gathering area were a middle school and a high school. It was within this community and within the local schools that ethnographic researchers spent minimally twenty hours per week for over a year getting to know many of the youths and peer groups.

FIELD WORK, SELECTION OF SAMPLE FOR INTERVIEWS[3,4]

During the first year, two field workers spent several hundred hours as ethnographic participant-observers (Bogdan and Taylor, 1975; Schatzman and Strauss, 1973; Glaser and Strauss, 1967; Cicourel, 1964), informally conversing with many youth and carefully observing and documenting the daily activities of youth in the study area. The field workers compiled information from ethnographic observations of approximately 700 youth in the community. Subsequently, a sample of 100 youth, ages 12 to 20, many of whom were involved in drugs and crime, was selected for purposes of in-depth interviewing during the period from June 1981 to June 1982.

To permit systematic comparisons of youth, three groups of subjects were chosen. First, forty youth were randomly selected from a list of all youth attending both the junior and the senior high schools in the study area. These subjects represented a cross section of youth in the community and served as a comparison group to two high-risk subsamples.

Second, the field workers purposively selected a group of forty youth known (by observations, conversation, or reputation) to be routinely or heavily involved in drugs and crime. Third, after extensive negotiation, permission was obtained from officials in the local juvenile system to conduct intensive interviews with youth incarcerated in the local juvenile detention facility or residing in group homes in the study area. These twenty subjects were adjudicated juvenile delinquents whom the courts and detention officers felt were among the most criminally involved youth in Yule City. Thus sixty youth who were highly involved in drugs and/or crime were interviewed, assuring extensive information about their life-styles, attitudes, and behaviors.

This plan for carefully selecting subjects for intensive study was designed to overcome a major problem that conventional surveys of the general population frequently encounter — that of obtaining only small numbers of highly involved persons despite a large sample size. For example, in a national sample of approximately 1,700 respondents, Huizinga (1982) found only about twenty respondents who reported committing twelve or more index offenses.

Analysis of the data from these subjects indicates that levels of drug use and crime were similar to rates that would be predicted by findings in larger national surveys of drug use by the adolescent population (Johnston et al., 1982). Similarly, despite a smaller sample size, the levels of drug use among the forty randomly selected youth were virtually identical to levels in a 1978 survey conducted in Yule City (ODAS, 1978). In short, the Yule City subjects selected randomly also appear very similar in their behaviors to other youth sampled in larger surveys.

INTERVIEWING, CODING, AND MAINFRAME COMPUTER RETRIEVAL[5]

An interview schedule was developed using the subjects' own terms, as these had come to be known through the field workers' efforts (Schwartz and Jacobs, 1979; Spradley, 1979; Cicourel, 1964). The resulting interview schedule consisted of 220 structured, open-ended questions and probes related to these, all of which were designed to concentrate on the subject's biography, with special focus on issues and events concerning peers, school activities and interests, religion, family background, and comprehensive discussion of involvement with alcohol, crime, and drugs (Frazier, 1978; Richardson et al., 1965; Becker and Geer, 1957).

Such an "in-depth" interview is the preferred format where the analyst seeks to understand the ways in which subjects themselves think and talk about the issues at hand, and where close rapport and acceptance between subject and interviewer is essential, given the sensitive nature of many of the topics discussed. The interviews did provide a wealth of information about subjects' activities and interests; why and how subjects became involved and continue to be involved in drugs, alcohol, and crime; the meanings they assigned to these behaviors; and how the behaviors changed over time.

The 100 subjects were intensively interviewed for three to eleven hours (mean of five hours) each. The interviews were conducted as conversations, with the questions designed to elicit extensive discussion about the subject's life, especially the areas concerning peers, school, activities and interests, family history, family, drug use, and crime. For reliability, focal topics were raised in more than one way and at different times in the discussion.

The interviews were tape recorded and transcribed verbatim onto computer tape, generating 90 to 300 transcript pages per subject. Using inductive analysis and the constant comparative method (Spradley, 1979; Bogdan and Taylor, 1975; Ostrander, 1970; Becker et al., 1968 and 1961; Glaser and Strauss, 1967 and 1966; Glaser, 1965), a detailed systematic codebook (Johnson et al., 1981) for cataloging the diverse contents of these transcripts was developed. This codebook contained forty-five major thematic topics, each assigned a numerical code; each major topic also had the possibility of ninety-nine minor codes (each also with a numerical code). Thus, each code was a four-digit number, analogous to a noun and its adjectival modifiers. The use of a four-digit code was a standardized procedure to enable retrieval of data via the computer program. Built into the coding catalogue and process was much redundancy, to improve the odds that relevant data could be retrieved, owing to inconsistencies in both subjects' accounts and coders' practices, and owing to the idiosyncrasies of analysts' retrieval practices.

Subsequently, each of the 100 transcripts was coded and catalogued according to theme by one of a dozen different coders supervised by the author. These codes were then entered into a computer program developed especially for this study.[6] This computerized retrieval system was designed to locate those pages, among the 15,000 to 20,000 total pages of transcripts, upon which a given code or combination of codes appeared; the retrieval system then could manage the printing out of the pages for analysis (Stuck and Glassner, 1982). The benefit of this particular retrieval process is that it maintains the integrity of the qualitative data by allowing the analyst to read discussions in context and at the same time permits access to the mass of data through use of the mainframe computer. However, given that the focal areas and coding scheme for the Yule City Study were much broader than the topic of interest in this current study, there was a need to develop an additional specialized coding and retrieval system to address the particular research questions of this study, described in Chapter 3.

NOTES

1. In part, this section was adopted from Johnson et al., 1982:5–8.
2. Ibid.
3. Ibid.
4. Ibid.
5. For those individuals who are concerned with the problems of "hired hand" research, the comments of Bogdan and Taylor (1975:92) and Bogdan and Biklen (1982:203) concerning observer bias and the role of team research in qualitative studies are especially helpful. Essentially, the point is made that the team approach to qualitative work allows the maximization of the research team (e.g., some individuals

are better interviewers than others; some are better writers) and also helps to mitigate researcher bias.

In terms of the Yule City Study, the interviewers were trained ethnographers in whom the research team had confidence; the coders were subjected to thorough and rigorous training by the author of this work; completed coding was checked by at least one member of the research team (also the author) for consistency and reliability; the mainframe data retrieval process had been subjected to many trials and refinements, which helped to maximize its use for analysis. Further, no interviewer could possibly remember all the nuances of the conversational interviews with each of the subjects, so concern that this author did not conduct interviews herself, and thus could not have access to such additional data, is not critical. In fact, by having had other researchers conduct the interviews, some of the researcher bias (see above) was automatically eliminated.

Finally, the author did not rely solely upon the Yule City Study's coding and retrieval process to access data; appropriate sections of transcripts were read in their entirety to ensure that richness of data had not been lost. In terms of the microcomputer data management process of coding and retrieval, since the codes were based upon the themes that emerged from the data, there was little danger of the codes dictating the findings. Also, since the themes were actually coded in two different places at two different times, verification and checking was possible. And lastly, the mainframe retrieval process was also used as a check against the microcomputer coding and retrieval.

6. This program used SAS statistical program, a language and syntax analyzer, and program generator for searching the codes and locating and printing the relevant transcript pages.

Bibliography

Adams, T., and H. Resnik. 1985. Teens in action: Creating a drug-free future for America's youth. Rockville, MD: National Institute on Drug Abuse.

Addams, J. 1974. *The spirit of youth and the city streets*. Reading, MA: Addison-Wesley Publishing.

Adler, P. T., and L. Lotecka. 1973. Drug use among high school students: Patterns and correlates. *The International Journal of the Addictions* 8((3):537–48.

Akers, R. L. 1977. *Deviant behavior: A social learning approach*. Belmont, CA: Wadsworth Publishing.

Akers, R. L., M. D. Krohn, L. Lanza-Kaduce, and M. Radosevich. 1979. Social learning and deviant behavior: A specific test of a general theory. *American Sociological Review* 44(Aug.):636–55.

American Alliance for Health, Physical Education and Recreation. 1954. *Resolutions. 58th national convention*. Washington, DC: AAHPER Publications.

American Association of School Administrators. 1985. Positive prevention: Successful approaches to preventing youthful drug and alcohol use (in English and Spanish). Arlington, VA: American Association of School Administrators.

Anderson, C. C. 1971. Drugs — America's current visible hysteria. *Journal of Drug Education* 1(4):391–99.

Andersen, M. L. 1983. *Thinking about women: Sociological and feminist perspectives*. New York: Macmillan.

Antonow, W. A., F. J. Eicke, and W. M. Mathews. 1976. Prevalent and preferred styles in drug education. *Journal of Drug Education* 6(2):117–25.

Baer, J., T. Jacobs, and F. Carr. 1975. Instructors' ratings of delinquents after outward bound survival training and their subsequent recidivism. *Psychological Reports* 36:547–53.

Bannister, R. 1973. The meaning of athletic performance. In *Sport and society: An anthology,* J. T. Talimini and C. H. Page, eds., 326–35. Boston: Little, Brown.

Barlow, H. D. 1984. *Introduction to criminology.* Boston: Little, Brown.

Barnes, C. P., and J. N. Olson. 1977. Usage patterns of nondrug alternatives in adolescence. *Journal of Drug Education* 7(4):359–68.

Baugh, R. J. 1970. The use and misuse of drugs among high school athletes. Washington, DC: U.S. Department of Health, Education and Welfare. National Institute of Education.

Becker, H. S. 1963. *Outsiders.* New York: Free Press.

____. 1958. Problems of inference and proof in participant observation. *American Sociological Review* 23:652–60.

Becker, H. S., and B. Geer. 1960. Participant observation: The analysis of qualitative field data. In *Human organization research,* R. N. Adams and J. J. Preiss, eds. Homewood, IL: Dorsey Press.

____. 1957. Participant observation and interviewing: A comparison. *Human Organization* 16:28–32.

Becker, H. S., B. Geer, and E. Hughes. 1968. *Making the grade.* New York: Wiley.

Becker, H. S., B. Geer, E. Hughes, and A. L. Strauss. 1961. *Boys in white: Student culture in medical school.* Chicago: University of Chicago Press.

Bedworth, D. A. 1971. Approaches to drug abuse prevention: Crusade vs. fact of life. *Journal of Drug Education* 1(3):285–91.

Belenky, M. F., B. M. Clinchy, N. R. Goldberger, and J. M. Tarule. 1986. *Women's ways of knowing.* New York: Basic Books.

Berg, B., M. Ksander, J. Loughlin, and B. Johnson. 1982. Full report version of cliques and groups: Adolescents, affective ties, and criminal activities. Unpublished paper. New York: Interdisciplinary Research Center.

Berryman, J. W. 1978. The rise of highly organized sports for pre-adolescent boys. In *Children in sport: A contemporary anthology,* R. A. Magill, M. J. Ash, and F. L. Smoll, eds., 3–18. Champaign, IL: Human Kinetics.

Best, J., and D. F. Luckenbill. 1982. *Organizing deviance*. Englewood Cliffs, NJ: Prentice-Hall.

Biddle, B. J., B. J. Bank, and M. M. Marlin. 1980a. Social determinants of adolescent drinking. *Journal of Studies on Alcohol* 41(3):215–41.

____. 1980b. Parental and peer influence on adolescents. *Social Forces* 58(4):1057–79.

Biddulph, L. G. 1954. Athletic attainment and the personal and social adjustment of high school boys. *Research Quarterly* 25:31–35.

Blount, W., and R. Dembo. 1984. Personal drug use and attitudes toward prevention among youth living in a high risk environment. *Journal of Drug Education* 14(3):207–25.

Blum, R. H., and Associates. 1970. *Students and drugs*. San Francisco: Jossey-Bass.

Bogdan, R. D., and S. K. Biklin. 1982. *Qualitative research for education: An introduction to theory and methods*. Boston: Allyn and Bacon.

Bogdan, R., and S. Taylor. 1975. *Introduction to qualitative research methods*. New York: Wiley.

Bonyun, R. 1981. *Survey of drug use in an Ottawa board high school*. Ottawa: Ottawa Board of Education (Ontario). Research Centre.

Bordua, D. 1960. *Sociological theories and their implications for juvenile delinquency*. Washington, DC: Government Printing Office.

Bouton, J. 1970. *Ball four: My life and hard times throwing the knuckleball in the big leagues*. New York: World.

Briar, S., and I. Piliavin. 1965. Delinquency, situational inducements, and commitment to conformity. *Social Problems* 13:35–45.

Brown, B. B. 1982. The extent and effects of peer pressure among high school students: A retrospective analysis. *Journal of Youth and Adolescence* 11(2):121–33.

Brown, J., and P. Finn. 1982. Drinking to get drunk: Findings of a survey of junior and senior high school students. *Journal of Alcohol and Drug Education* 27(3):13–25.

Buhrman, H. G. 1977. Athletics and deviance: An examination of the relationship between participation and deviant behavior of high school girls. *Review of Sport and Leisure* 2(June):17–35.

Buhrman, H. G., and R. D. Bratton. 1978. Athletic participation and deviant behavior of high school girls in Alberta. *Review of Sport and Leisure* 3(2):25–41.

Butler, G. D. 1976. *Introduction to community recreation.* New York: McGraw-Hill.

Chase, N. K. 1981. Outward bound as an adjunct to therapy. Colorado Outward Bound School, 21 pp.

Cicourel, A. 1964. *Method and measurement in sociology.* New York: Free Press.

Clinard, M., and A. Wade. 1966. Juvenile delinquency. In *Readings in juvenile delinquency,* R. S. Cavan, ed. New York: J. B. Lippincott.

Cloward, R. A., and L. E. Ohlin. 1960. *Delinquency and opportunity: A theory of delinquent gangs.* New York: The Free Press.

Coakley, J. J. 1978. *Sport in society.* St. Louis: C. V. Mosby.

Cohen, A., and J. Short. 1958. Research on delinquent subcultures. *American Sociological Review* 14:20–31.

Cohen, A. K. 1955. *Delinquent boys: The culture of the gang.* New York: The Free Press.

Cohen, A. Y. 1973. *Alternatives to drug abuse: Steps toward prevention.* Rockville, MD: National Institute on Drug Abuse.

Coleman, J. S. 1965. *Adolescents and the schools.* New York: Basic Books.

_____. 1961a. *The adolescent society.* New York: The Free Press.

_____. 1961b. Athletics in high school. *Annals of the American Academy of Political and Social Science* 338:33–43.

Conger, R. D. 1980. Juvenile delinquency: Behavior restraint or behavior facilitation. In *Understanding crime: Current theory and research,* Vol. 18, Sage Research Progress Series in Criminology, T. Hirschi and M. Gottfredson, eds. Beverly Hills: Sage.

Cortland Standard. 1989. Study provides glimpses of teens' psyche. February 23, p. 21.

Cowell, C. C., and A. H. Ismail. 1962. Relationships between selected social and physical factors. *Research Quarterly* 33:40–43.

Donnelly, P. 1981a. Athletes and juvenile delinquents: A comparative analysis based on a review of the literature. *Adolescence* 16(62):421–32.

_____. 1981b. Toward a definition of sport subcultures. In *Sport in the sociocultural process,* 3rd ed., M. Hart and S. Birrell, eds. 565–87. Dubuque, IA: Wm. C. Brown.

Eckert, P. 1989. *Jocks & burnouts: Social categories and identity in the high school.* New York: Teachers College Press.

Educational Policies Commission. 1964. *School athletics: Problems and policies.* Washington, DC: U.S. Government Printing Office.

Edwards, H. 1973. *Sociology of sport.* Homewood, IL: Dorsey Press.

Elliott, D. S., D. Huizinga, and S. S. Ageton. 1985. *Explaining delinquency and drug use.* Beverly Hills: Sage.

Empey, L. T. 1982, 1978. *American delinquency: Its meaning and construction.* Homewood, IL: Dorsey Press.

Erikson, E. 1968. *Identity, youth and crisis.* New York: W. W. Norton.

Everhart, R. B. 1982. The nature of "goofing off" among junior high school adolescents. *Adolescence* 17(65):177–88.

Fagerberg, S., and K. Fagerberg. 1976. Student attitudes concerning drug abuse education and prevention. *Journal of Drug Education* 6(2):141–52.

Ferdinand, T. N. 1966. *Typologies of delinquency: A critical analysis.* New York: Random House.

Fichter, J. H. 1961. *Parochial school: A sociological study.* Garden City, NY: Anchor Books.

Figler, S. 1981. *Sport and play in American life.* New York: CBS College Publishing.

Forslund, M. A., and T. J. Gustafson. 1970. Influence of peers and parents and sex differences in drinking by high-school students. *Quarterly Journal of Studies on Alcohol* 31:868–75.

Frazier, C. 1978. The use of life-histories in testing theories of criminal behavior. *Qualitative Sociology* 1:122–42.

Friedenberg, E. 1973. The adolescent and high school athletics. In *Sport and society: An anthology,* J. T. Talamini and C. H. Page, eds., 182–88. Boston: Little, Brown.

Fritzen, R. D., and G. E. Mazer. 1975. The effects of fear appeal and a communication upon attitudes toward alcohol consumption. *Journal of Drug Education* 5(2):171–81.

Gaus, C. 1981. Experiential education as an integral part of day treatment for adjudicated delinquent youth. Paper presented at the Annual Conference of the Association of Experiential Education. Toronto, Canada.

Gibbs, J. P. 1981. Norms and deviance. In *Norms, deviance and social control: Conceptual matters,* J. P. Gibbs, ed., 1–181. New York: Elsevier.

Gilligan, C. 1982. *In a different voice.* Cambridge, MA: Harvard University Press.

Ginsberg, I. J., and J. R. Greenley. 1978. Competing theories of marijuana use: A longitudinal study. *Journal of Health and Social Behavior* 19:22–34.

Glaser, B. G. 1965. The constant comparative method of qualitative analysis. *Social Problems* 12(4):436–45.

Glaser, B. G., and A. S. Strauss. 1967. *The discovery of grounded theory.* Chicago: Aldine.

____. 1966. The purpose and credibility of qualitative research. *Nursing Research* 15(1):56–61.

Glueck, S., and E. Glueck. 1950. *Unraveling juvenile delinquency.* New York: Commonwealth Fund.

Gold, M. 1970. *Delinquent behavior in an American city.* Belmont, CA: Wadsworth.

Gordon, C. W. 1957. *The social system of the high school.* New York: The Free Press.

Guinn, R. 1975. Characteristics of drug use among Mexican-American students. *Journal of Drug Education* 5(3):235–41.

Haines, M. P. 1983. Eat, drink and be merry: Signs and symptoms of alcohol wellness. Paper presented at Annual Meeting of the American College Health Association, St. Louis, MO.

Hammersley, M. 1981. Using qualitative methods. *Social Science Information Studies* 1(4):209–20.

Hanks, M. 1981. Youth, voluntary associations and political socialization. *Social Forces* 60(1):211–23.

Hawkins, J. D., D. M. Lishner, R. F. Catalano, Jr., and M. O. Howard. 1985. Childhood predictors of adolescent substance abuse: Toward an empirically grounded theory. *Journal of Children in Contemporary Society* 18(2):11–48.

Hayes, R. W., and B. W. Tevis. 1977. A comparison of attitudes and behavior of high school athletes and non-athletes with respect to alcohol use and abuse. *Journal of Alcohol and Drug Education* 23(Fall):20–28.

Healy, W., and B. S. Alper. 1941. *Criminal youth and the Borstal system*. New York: Commonwealth Fund.

Hewitt, J. P., and R. Stokes. 1975. Disclaimers. *American Sociological Review* 40(1):1–11.

Hills, S. L. 1980. *Demystifying social deviance*. New York: McGraw-Hill.

Hindelang, M. J. 1973. Causes of delinquency: A partial replication and extension. *Social Problems* 20(4):471–87.

Hindelang, M. J., T. Hirschi, and J. G. Weis. 1979. Correlates of delinquency: The illusion of discrepancy between self-report and official measures. *American Sociological Review* 44(Dec.):995–1014.

Hirschi, T. 1969. *Causes of delinquency*. Berkeley: University of California Press.

Hobfall, S. E., and B. Segal. 1983. A factor analytic study of the relationship of experience seeking and trait anxiety to drug use and reasons for drug use. *International Journal of the Addictions* 18(4):539–49.

Hollingshead, A. 1949. *Elmtown's youth*. New York: Wiley.

Holsti, O. P. 1969. *Content analysis for the social sciences and humanities*. Reading, MA: Addison-Wesley.

Huba, G. J., J. A. Wingard, and P. M. Butler. 1979. Beginning adolescent drug use and peer and adult interaction patterns. *Journal of Consulting and Clinical Psychology* 47(2):265–76.

Huizinga, D. 1982. *The relationship between criminal and drug use behavior in a national sample of youth*. New York: Interdisciplinary Research Center, and Boulder, CO: Behavioral Research Institute.

Jackson, M., and B. Jackson. 1983. *Doing drugs*. New York: St. Martin's/Marek.

Jessor, R. 1982. Problem behavior and developmental transition in adolescence. *Journal of School Health* (Kent) 52(5):295–300.

Jessor, R., and S. L. Jessor. 1977. *Problem behavior and psychosocial development — A longitudinal study of youth*. New York: Academic Press.

Johnson, B. D., B. Glassner, D. Strug, and M. F. Stuck. 1981. *Variable field codebook*. New York: Interdisciplinary Research Center.

Johnson, B. D., B. Glassner, and E. Wish. 1982. *Application for year 3 funding to the National Institute of Justice*. New York: Interdisciplinary Research Center.

Johnson, C., W. B. Hansen, J. W. Graham, B. R. Flay, and M. A. Pentz. 1986. Project SMART: A social approach to drug abuse prevention — teacher's guide. Los Angeles: University of Southern California, Los Angeles.

Johnson, D. 1980. Group processes: Influences of student-student interaction on school outcome. In *The social psychology of school learning,* J. McMillan, ed. New York: Academic Press.

Johnson, R. E. 1979. *Juvenile delinquency and its origins: An integrated theoretical approach.* New York: Cambridge University Press.

Johnstone, J. W. C. 1981. Youth gangs and black suburbs. *Pacific Sociological Review* 24(July):355–75.

Kandel, D. B. 1980. Drugs and drinking behavior among youth. *Annual Review of Sociology* 6:235–85.

____. 1974a. Inter and intragenerational influences on adolescent marijuana use. *Journal of Social Issues* 30(2):107–35.

____. 1974b. Interpersonal influence on adolescent illegal drug use. In *Drug use: Epidemiological and sociological approaches,* E. Josephson and E. E. Carroll, eds. Washington, DC: Hemisphere.

Kandel, D., R. C. Kessler, and R. S. Margulies. 1978. Antecedents of adolescent initiation into states of drug use: A developmental analysis. *Journal of Youth and Adolescence* 7:13–40.

Kaplan, H. B., S. Martin, and C. Robbins. 1984. Pathways to adolescent drug use: Self-derogation, peer influence, weakening of social controls, and early substance use. *Journal of Health and Social Behavior* 25(3):270–89.

Kelly, J., and J. Baer. 1971. Psychological challenge as a treatment for delinquency. *Crime and Delinquency* 17:437–45.

Kenyon, G. S., and B. D. McPherson. 1981. Becoming involved in physical activity and sport: A process of socialization. In *Sport, culture and society: A reader on the sociology of sport,* J. W. Loy, Jr., G. S. Kenyon, B. D. McPherson, eds., 217–37. Philadelphia: Lea and Febiger.

Kitsuse, J. I., and D. C. Dietrick. 1959. Delinquent boys: A critique. *American Sociological Review* 24(April):213–15.

Kohlberg, L. 1981. *The philosophy of moral development.* San Francisco: Harper and Row.

Konopka, G. 1973. Requirements for healthy development of adolescent youth. *Adolescence* 8(31):1–26.

Krippendorff, K. 1980. *Content analysis: An introduction to its methodology.* Beverly Hills: Sage.

Krohn, M. D., and J. L. Massey. 1980. Social control and delinquent behavior: An examination of the elements of the social bond. *Sociological Quarterly* 21(Autumn):529–44.

Kwakman, A. M., F. A. J. M. Zuiker, G. M. Schippers, and F. J. de Wuffel. 1988. Drinking behavior, drinking attitudes, and attachment relationships of adolescents. *Journal of Youth and Adolescence* 17(3):247–53.

Landers, D. M., and D. M. Landers. 1977. Socialization via interscholastic athletics: Its effect on delinquency. *Sociology of Education* 51:229–303.

Lazarsfeld, P. F., and A. H. Barton. 1955. Some functions of qualitative analysis in sociological research. *Sociologica* 1:324–61.

Lee, R. E., and H. M. Schroder. 1969. Effects of Outward Bound training on urban youth. *Journal of Special Education* 3(2):187–205.

LeMonn, J. 1987. First Lady Nancy Reagan tells Ayassiz village campers to "Just say no" to drugs. *Camping Magazine* 60(1):11–13.

Leonard, W. M., II. 1984. *A sociological perspective of sports.* Minneapolis: Burgess.

Levine, E. M., and C. Kozak, 1979. Drug and alcohol use, delinquency, and vandalism among upper middle class pre- and post-adolescents. *Journal of Youth and Adolescents* 8(1):91–101.

Lohrman, D. K., and S. W. Fors. 1986. Can school-based educational programs really be expected to solve the adolescent drug abuse problem? *Journal of Drug Education* 16(4):327–39.

Loy, J. W. 1968. The study of sport and social mobility. In *Aspects of contemporary sport sociology,* G. Kenyon, ed. Chicago: The Athletic Institute.

Loy, J. W., G. S. Kenyon, and B. D. McPherson. 1981. *Sport, culture and society,* 2nd ed. Philadelphia: Lea & Febiger.

Lucas, W. L., S. E. Grup, and R. L. Schmitt. 1975. Predicting who will turn on: A four-year follow-up. *International Journal of the Addictions* 10:305–26.

Lueschen, G. R. F. 1976. Cheating in sport. In *Social problems in athletics,* D. M. Landers, ed., 67–77. Urbana-Champaign: University of Illinois Press.

Lueschen, G. R. F., and G. H. Sage, eds. 1981. *Handbook of social science of sport.* Champaign, IL: Stipes Publishing.

Lynd, R. S., and H. M. Lynd. 1929. *Middletown.* New York: Harcourt, Brace and Co.

Mathews, W. M. 1975. A critique of traditional drug education programs. *Journal of Drug Education* 5(1):58–64.

Matza, D. 1969. *Becoming deviant.* Englewood Cliffs, NJ: Prentice-Hall.

____. 1964a. *Delinquency and drift.* New York: John Wiley.

____. 1964b. Position and behavior patterns of youth. In *Handbook of modern sociology,* R. E. L. Faris, ed. Chicago: Rand McNally.

McCall, G. J., and J. L. Simmons. 1969. *Issues in participant observation.* Reading, MA: Addison-Wesley.

McCann, H. G., R. A. Steffenhagen, and G. Merriam. 1977. Drug use: A model for a deviant sub-culture. *Journal of Alcohol and Drug Education* 23(1):29–45.

McIntosh, P. C. 1971. An historical view of sport and social control. *International Review of Sport Sociology* 6:5–16.

McPherson, B. D. 1981. Socialization into and through sport involvement. In *Handbook of social science of sport,* G. R. F. Lueschen, and G. W. Sage, eds., 246–73. Champaign, IL: Stipes Publishing.

Meade, A. C., and M. E. Marsden. 1981. An integration of classic theories of delinquency. In *Youth and society studies of adolescent deviance,* A. C. Meade, ed. Chicago: Institute for Juvenile Research.

Meier, R. F. 1982. Perspectives on the concept of social control. *Annual Review of Sociology* 8:35–55.

Mensch, B. S., and D. B. Kandel. 1988. Dropping out of high school and drug involvement. *Sociology of Education* 61(April):95–113.

Messolonghites, L., ed. 1974. *Alternative pursuits for America's 3rd century: A resource book on new perceptions, processes, and programs — with implications for the prevention of drug abuse.* Rockville, MD: National Institute on Drug Abuse.

Mills, C. W. 1959. *The sociological imagination.* London: Oxford University Press.

____. 1940. Situated actions and vocabularies of motive. *American Sociological Review* 9(Dec.):940–13.

Minatoya, L. Y., and W. E. Sedlacek. 1979. *A new look at freshmen attitudes and behavior towards drugs.* College Park, MD: University of Maryland, Office of Vice Chancellor for Student Affairs, Counseling Center.

Mitchell, J., and R. A. Dodder. 1983. Types of neutralization and types of delinquency. *Journal of Youth and Adolescence* 12(4):307–18.

Montgomery County Drug Commission. 1971. *Drug abuse*. Norristown, PA: Montgomery County Drug Commission.

Moos, R. H., B. S. Moos, and J. A. Kulik. 1976. College student abstainers, moderate drinkers, and heavy drinkers: A comparative analysis. *Journal of Youth and Adolescence* 5(Dec.):349–60.

New York Times. 1985. What happens when beer and wine and television mix? May 26, D16.

Nolan, J. B. 1955. Athletics and juvenile delinquency. *Journal of Educational Sociology* 28:263–65.

Norem-Hebeisen, A., and D. Hedin. 1981. Influences on adolescent problem behavior: Causes, connections, and contexts. In *Adolescent peer pressure: Theory, correlates, and program implications to drug abuse prevention (NIDA)*. Washington, DC: U.S. Government Printing Office.

Novak, M. 1976. *The joy of sports*. New York: Basic Books.

O'Connor, C. 1976. Exorcising boredom. *Parks and Recreation* 11(11):31–34.

ODAS. 1978. *Substance use among New York State public and parochial school students in grades 7 through 12*. Albany, NY: New York State Office of Drug Abuse Services.

Orr, J. 1969. *The black athlete: His story in American history*. New York: Lion Press.

Ostrander, S. A. 1970. Grounded theory: The method of discovery. *Case Western Reserve Journal of Sociology* 4(Dec.):29–42.

Pearson, K. 1981. Subcultures and sport. In *Sport, culture and society*, 2nd ed., J. W. Loy, G. S. Kenyon, B. D. McPherson, eds. Philadelphia: Lea & Febiger.

Phillips, J. C., and W. E. Schafer. 1971. Consequences of participation in interscholastic athletics: A review and prospectus. *Pacific Sociological Review* 14(July):328–38.

Pickens, K. 1985. The young and the volatile: Coping with solvent abuse. New Zealand Council for Educational Research, 48 pp.

Pisano, S., and J. F. Rooney. 1988. Children's changing attitudes regarding alcohol: A cross-sectional study. *Journal of Drug Education* 18(1):1–11.

Purdy, D. A., and S. F. Richard. 1983. Sport and juvenile delinquency: An examination and assessment of four major theories. *Journal of Sport Behavior* 6(4):179–93.

Rehberg, R. A. 1971. Preliminary data: NIMH 1925. Unpublished paper. Binghamton, NY: SUNY-Binghamton Department of Sociology.

_____. 1969. Behavioral and attitudinal consequences of high school interscholastic sports: A speculative consideration. *Adolescence* 4(13):69–88.

Research & Forecasts, Inc. 1983. *The Miller Lite report on American attitudes towards sports.* Milwaukee: Miller Brewing Company.

Resnik, H. S., and J. Gibbs. 1981. Types of peer program approaches. In *Adolescent peer pressure: Theory, correlates, and program implications for drug abuse prevention (NIDA),* 47–89. Washington, DC: U.S. Government Printing Office.

Rhoden, W. C. 1984. School chancellor offers sport as an answer to dropout rate. *New York Times,* January 8, p. 53.

Richardson, S., B. S. Dohrenwend, and D. Klein. 1965. *Interviewing: Its form and function.* New York: Basic Books.

Rooney, J. F. 1984. Sports and clean living: A useful myth? *Drug and Alcohol Dependence* 13:75–87.

_____. 1982–83. The influence of informal control sources upon adolescent alcohol use and problems. *American Journal of Drug Alcohol Abuse* 9(2):233–45.

Rubington, E., and M. S. Weinberg. 1981. *Deviance: The interactionist perspective,* 4th ed. New York: Macmillan.

Rugg, C., and J. H. Jaynes. 1983. The role of chemical abuse during adolescence. *Focus on Alcohol and Drug Issues* 6(3):16–17, 27.

Rutter, M., and H. Giller. 1983. *Juvenile delinquency: Trends and perspectives.* New York: Guilford Press.

Ryan, W. 1976. *Blaming the victim.* New York: Vintage Books.

Samuels, D. J., and M. Samuels. 1974. Low self-concept as a cause of drug abuse. *Journal of Drug Education* 4(4):421–36.

Santomier, J. P., W. G. Howard, W. L. Plitze, and T. J. Romance. 1980. White sock crime: Organizational deviance in intercollegiate athletics. *Journal of Sport and Social Issues* 4(2):26–32.

Sarvela, P. D., and E. J. McClendon. 1983. Correlates of early adolescent peer and personal substance use in rural northern Michigan. *Journal of Youth and Adolescence* 12(4):319–22.

Schafer, W. E. 1971. Sport, socialization and the school: Toward maturity or enculturation? Paper presented at the Third International Symposium on the Sociology of Sport. Waterloo, Ontario, Canada.

_____. 1969a. Participation in interscholastic athletics and delinquency: A preliminary study. *Social Problems* 17:40–47.

_____. 1969b. Some social sources and consequences of interscholastic athletics: The case of participation and delinquency. *International Review of Sport Sociology* 4:63–82.

Schafer, W. E., and M. J. Armer. 1968. Athletes are not inferior students. *Transaction* 6:21–26, 61–62.

Schatzman, L., and A. Strauss. 1973. *Field research.* Englewood Cliffs: Prentice Hall.

Schutz, A. 1962. Concept and theory formation in the social sciences. In *Collected papers I. The problem of social reality,* M. Natanson, ed., 48–66. The Hague: Martinus Nijhoff.

Schwartz, H., and J. Jacobs. 1979. *Qualitative sociology.* New York: Free Press.

Scott, J. 1971. *The athletic revolution.* New York: Macmillan.

Scott, M. B., and S. M. Lyman. 1968. Accounts. *American Sociological Review* 33(1):46–62.

Seffrin, J. R., and R. W. Seehafer. 1976. A survey of drug use beliefs, opinions and behavior among junior and senior high school students. *Journal of School Health* 46(5):263–68.

Segal, B. 1977. Reasons for marijuana use and personality: A canonical analysis. *Journal of Alcohol and Drug Education* 2(3):64–67.

Segal, B., G. J. Huba, and J. L. Singer. 1980. *Drugs, daydreaming and personality: A study of college youth.* Hillsdale, NJ: Erlbaum Associates.

Segal, B., J. McKelvy, D. Bowman, and T. Mala. 1983. Patterns of drug use: School survey. Alaska State Office of Alcoholism and Drug Abuse, 273 pp.

Segrave, J. O. 1983. Sport and juvenile delinquency. In *Exercise and sport science reviews,* Vol. 11, *American College of Sports Medicine Journal,* R. L. Terjung, ed. Philadelphia: The Franklin Institute.

_____. 1981a. *An investigation into the relationship between participation in interscholastic athletics and delinquent behavior.* Ph.D. dissertation. Tempe, AZ: Arizona State University.

_____. 1981b. Juvenile delinquency and athletics: The deterrent hypothesis. Paper presented at the Symposium on Athletics and Delinquency at the Second Annual Convention for the Sociology of Sport. Fort Worth, TX, Nov. 14–17, 1981.

Segrave, J. O., and D. B. Chu. 1978. Athletics and juvenile delinquency. *Review of Sport and Leisure* 3(2):1–24.

Segrave, J. O., and D. N. Hastad. 1982. Delinquent behavior and interscholastic athletic participation. *Journal of Sport Behavior* 5(2):96–111.

Selakovich, D. 1984. *Schooling in America.* New York: Longman.

Shearn, C. R., and D. J. Fitzgibbons. 1973. Survey of reasons for illicit drug use in a population of youthful psychiatric inpatients. *International Journal of the Addictions* 8:623–33.

Sheppard, M. A. 1980. Sources of information about drugs. *Journal of Drug Education* 10(3):257–62.

Shibutani, T. 1955. Reference groups as perspectives. *American Journal of Sociology* 60:562.

Short, J. F., and F. L. Strodtbeck. 1965. *Group process and gang delinquency.* Chicago: University of Chicago Press.

Siegel, L. J., and J. J. Senna. 1981. *Juvenile delinquency: Theory, practice, and law,* 2nd ed. St. Paul, MN: West Publishing.

Silverman, W. H. 1987. Guidelines for competence and skills development for substance abuse prevention. Paper presented at the Annual Meeting of the Southeastern Psychological Association. Atlanta, GA.

Simon, D. R., and D. S. Eitzen. 1982. *Elite deviance.* Boston: Allyn and Bacon.

Snyder, E. E. 1972. Athletic dressing room slogans as folklore: A means of socialization. *International Review of Sport Sociology* 7:89–107.

Snyder, E. E. and E. Spreitzer. 1980. Sport, education, and schools. In *Handbook of social science of sport,* G. R. F. Lueschen and G. H. Sage, eds., 119–46. Champaign, IL: Stipes Publishing.

_____. 1979. High school value climate as related to preferential treatment of athletes. *Research Quarterly* 50(3):460–67.

_____. 1974. Sociology of sport: An overview. *Sociological Quarterly* (Autumn):467–87.

Spady, W. G. 1971. Status, achievement and motivation in the American high school. *School Review* 79(May):379–403.

Spradley, J. 1979. *The ethnographic interview.* New York: Holt, Rinehart and Winston.

Stanley, L., and S. Wise. 1983. *Breaking out: Feminist consciousness and feminist research.* London: Routledge & Kegan Paul.

Stevenson, C. L., and J. E. Nixon. 1972. A conceptual scheme of the social functions of sport. *Sportwissenschaft* 2:119–32.

Stodgill, R. M. 1948. Personality factors associated with leadership. *Journal of Psychology* 25:35–71.

Strong, J. 1907. *The challenge of the city.* New York: Charles Scribner's Sons.

Stuck, M. F., and B. Glassner, 1982. A computerized coding and retrieval system for qualitative data analysis. Unpublished paper.

Sugden, J., and A. Yiannakis. 1982. Sport and juvenile delinquency: A theoretical base. *Journal of Sport and Social Issues* 6(1):22–30.

Sutherland, E. H. 1939. *Principles of criminology.* Philadelphia: Lippincott.

Sutherland, E. H., and D. R. Cressey. 1955. *Principles of Criminology,* 5th ed. Philadelphia: Lippincott.

Sykes, G. M., and D. Matza. 1957. Techniques of neutralization: A theory of delinquency. *American Sociological Review* 22:664–70.

Tappan, P. W. 1949. *Juvenile delinquency.* New York: McGraw-Hill.

Tec, N. 1972. Some aspects of high school status and differential involvement with marijuana: A study of suburban teenagers. *Adolescence* 7(Spring):1–28.

Thomas, C. W., and J. M. Hyman. 1978. Compliance theory, control theory and juvenile delinquency. In *Crime, law and sanctions,* M. D. Krohn and R. L. Akers, eds., 73–90. Beverly Hills: Sage.

Thompson, R. 1977. *Sport and deviance: A subcultural analysis.* Ph.D. dissertation. Edmonton: University of Alberta.

____. 1964. *Race and sport.* London: Oxford University Press.

Thrasher, F. M. 1963. *The gang.* Chicago: University of Chicago Press.

U.S. Senate Committee on Governmental Affairs. 1985. The role of the entertainment industry in deglamorizing drug use. Hearing before the permanent subcommittee on investigations of the committee on governmental affairs. United States Senate. Ninety-Ninth Congress, First Session.

Varenhorst, B. 1981. The adolescent society. In *Adolescent peer pressure: Theory, correlates, and program implications for drug abuse prevention* (NIDA). Washington, DC: U.S. Government Printing Office.

Waller, W. W. 1965. *The sociology of teaching.* New York: John Wiley.

Wasson, A. S. 1981. Susceptibility to boredom and deviant behavior at school. *Psychological Reports* 48:901–2.

Weinstein, R. M. 1980. Vocabularies of motive for illicit drug use: An application of the accounts framework. *Sociological Quarterly* 21(Autumn):577–93.

Wiatrowski, M. D., D. B. Griswold, and M. K. Roberts. 1981. Social control theory and delinquency. *American Sociological Review* 46(Oct.):525–41.

Wichmann, T. F. 1983. Evaluating Outward Bound for delinquent youth. *Journal of Experiential Education* 5(3):10–16.

Williams, R., D. A. Ward, L. N. Gray. 1985. The persistence of experimentally induced cognitive change: A neglected dimension in the assessment of drug prevention programs. *Journal of Drug Education* 15(1):33–42.

Wiseman, J. 1974. The research web. *Urban Life and Culture* 3(3):317–28.

Wolf, D. 1972. *Foul: The Connie Hawkins story.* New York: Warner.

Yiannakis, A. 1981. Athletics, delinquency, and the deterrence hypothesis. Paper presented at the Second Annual Convention of the North American Society for the Sociology of Sport, Fort Worth, TX.

_____. 1980. Sport and delinquency: A review and appraisal. *Motor Skills* 4(1):59–64.

Index

ABOUT THE AUTHOR

M. F. STUCK received degrees from The Ohio State University and Syracuse University and has taught Sociology and Public Justice in New York state colleges for the past ten years. Currently Dr. Stuck is an Assistant Professor of Sociology and Public Justice at State University of New York at Oswego.

Some of the author's work in the same area as this book has been published in *Adolescence* and *The ARENA Review*. In addition a co-authored case study based on some of the Yule City data was published as a chapter in Carpenter, et al. (eds.), *Kids, Drugs and Crime*.

The author has also made numerous presentations on this topic at national and international meetings for groups such as American Educational Research Association; Eastern Sociological Society; American Alliance for Health, Physical Education, Recreation and Dance; and the Fifth Canadian Congress on Leisure Research.